RAILWAY
ADVENTURE

RAILWAY
ADVENTURE

L.T.C. ROLT

ALAN SUTTON

First published 1953

First published in this edition in the United Kingdom in 1993
Alan Sutton Publishing Ltd · Phoenix Mill · Far Thrupp · Stroud
Gloucestershire

British Library Cataloguing in Publication Data

Rolt, L.T.C. (Lionel Thomas Caswell)
Railway Adventure.
I. Title
385.520942929

ISBN 0-86299-367-9

Typeset in 11/14 Bembo.
Typesetting and origination by
Alan Sutton Publishing Limited.
Printed and bound in Great Britain by
Butler & Tanner Ltd, Frome and London

Contents

INTRODUCTION   page vii

ACKNOWLEDGEMENTS   page xi

ACKNOWLEDGEMENTS FOR NEW EDITION   page xiii

FOREWORD   page xv

CHAPTER ONE   page 1

CHAPTER TWO   page 28

CHAPTER THREE   page 47

CHAPTER FOUR   page 76

CHAPTER FIVE   page 117

to
W.G. TRINDER
AND
J.S. RUSSELL
PARTNERS IN ADVENTURE

Introduction

Since its first publication in 1953, Tom Rolt's *Railway Adventure* has become a classic. It is a very full and fair account of the first two years of the world's first successful take-over and restoration of a moribund railway by enthusiasts and volunteers. The main object of the book at the time was, of course, to help publicise and assist the Talyllyn Railway Preservation Society's cause. In this it succeeded. Before 1953, although with enormous efforts we were beginning to stem the tide, the balance of increasing dilapidations against growing traffic was still swinging against us. After the book appeared, the tide began to turn. Nowadays the Talyllyn Railway is a neat and tidy, apple-pie-order operation. Although the original locomotives and rolling-stock are still running, much has been added and it is hard to imagine now just how decrepit and overwhelmed things were.

In the book, Tom Rolt (for perfectly good reasons) did not go too deeply into some matters; for instance, the extent to which parts of DOLGOCH'S boiler plates had wasted away. This was not discovered till later, though this particular item did not greatly surprise those of us who used to sit around the engine at midday, eating sandwiches as we listened to the water bubbling and boiling gently inside. Another thing was the cumulative nervous tension of operating such run-down equipment, which had begun to tell on us by each September. But every winter the worst problems were tackled, and spirits rose again as one by one they disappeared.

I do not think any of us quite realised what we were starting. I certainly had a typical teenager's cause myself: if we could hold the fort at such a threatened outpost as the Talyllyn Railway, surely nobody would have the arrogance to dream of closing such useful branches as those to places like Tenterden, or Bellingham (North

Tyne), let alone important main lines like the Somerset & Dorset. Tom's cause was, as it turned out, more realistic and achievable: to reverse the fashion to centralise and nationalise; to restore the tradition of self-supporting local concerns in which people could take a legitimate pride of achievement. To get away from conformity and dependence. In fact, to work towards some of the ideals that later grouped under the banner 'Small is Beautiful', but more than that: to enlarge the duty, and the joy, of living.

The world has begun to change, and it is moving now in Tom's direction. Sometimes it takes only a small stone falling to start an avalanche. Nearly forty years on, it looks as if Tom Rolt, with that small group he led at Towyn in 1951 and 1952, may have started to move that first stone. If this seems a large claim to make, founded on nothing more than a mildly ridiculous and no-longer-needed, long-funnelled, old Welsh narrow-gauge railway, and some absurd nutters who would not let it die, just stop for a minute and look around you.

J.B. SNELL
April 1992

Author's Note and Acknowledgements

I am deeply indebted to all those who supplied the photographs which illustrate this book and to Mr James Boswell for his generosity in enabling me to make use of his delightful drawings. The names of the photographers, the majority of whom are members of the Talyllyn Railway Preservation Society, are individually acknowledged on the relevant plates.

I would also acknowledge my indebtedness to the Ministry of Transport for enabling me to quote Captain H. W. Tyler's Reports and to Mr Siegfried Sassoon for so kindly permitting me to quote a part of his poem 'A Local Train of Thought'. As it in no way interfered with the metre but rounded the aptness of the quotation I have altered the time of Mr Sassoon's train from one-fifty to two-fifty in order to agree with the Talyllyn Railway time-table and hope the author will accept my apology for this liberty.

I would stress the fact that this is a personal book which means that the opinions expressed in it do not necessarily represent the views or the policy of the Talyllyn Railway Company or of the Talyllyn Railway Preservation Society. I am, none the less, most deeply indebted to all those railwaymen, amateur and professional, who came forward to play practical and creative parts in this railway adventure. For had it not been for their boundless enthusiasm and their unwearying labours at Towyn there would have been no story for me to write.

One brief explanatory footnote. Some readers may comment upon the fact that I have referred to locomotives bearing masculine names as 'she'. I am sure that all locomotive men will agree with me when I say that a machine so individual in character as the steam locomotive, so temperamental and cussed at times and yet withal so fascinating and responsive cannot possibly be assigned the masculine gender. So I hope I shall be forgiven this apparent inconsistency.

L.T.C.R.

Acknowledgements for New Edition

For this edition, since not all the original photographs were available, gratitude is owed to a number of institutions or people who have lent duplicates or kindly provided alternatives taken by them or from their own collections. As a general rule the intention has been to follow the text closely with either a contemporary picture or one representing a similar scene. Wherever possible both photographer and atribution is given. In some cases it has not been possible to get in touch with the early photographers (for instance for the evocative work of Michael Peto) and apologies are offered to anyone who has been overlooked. Grateful thanks are due to The Talyllyn Railway Archive, *The Times*, the *Daily Express*, The Hulton Deutsch Collection Limited, British Rail photographic department and the Rolt Archive. For advice and help and further loans without which the illustrations would have been sadly diminished thanks are also due to J.I.C. Boyd, John Snell, John Adams, Patrick Whitehouse, Robin Butterell, J.G. Vincent, Bill Harvey, David Woodhouse, J.J. Davis, J.C. Flemons, L.T. Catchpole and Michael Howard, Archivist to the Talyllyn Railway.

SONIA ROLT, 1993

I hear a local train along the Valley. And 'There
Goes the two-fifty,' think I to myself; aware
That somehow its habitual travelling comforts me,
Making my world seem safer, homelier, sure to be
The same to-morrow; and the same, one hopes, next year.
'There's peacetime in that train.' One hears it disappear
With needless warning whistle and rail-resounding wheels.
'That train's quite like an old familiar friend,' one feels.

SIEGFRIED SASSOON

Road to adventure

Foreword

This book is both encouraging and interesting. It has a twofold appeal. First it is a remarkable story of disinterested enterprise. You will find in these pages the account of Mr Rolt's first visit to the Talyllyn Railway, the abrupt notice 'NO TRAIN TO-DAY', and his walk along the grassy, silent track among the mountains, and his discovery of the ancient engines and rolling-stock. You will read of his visit to that splendid octogenarian owner of the line, Sir Haydn Jones, sitting in his eyrie above Towyn Post Office and still wearing the pin-stripe trousers and frock coat of an old-fashioned MP. You will hear of how Sir Haydn said that although he was losing money on the line, he would keep the summer services going so long as he was alive, and how on his death, with the help of Mr Edward Thomas and Lady Haydn Jones, Mr Rolt and his friends raised the money and the labour to put the line into working order, and how it now carries thousands of excursionists along its beautiful seven miles of track, during the summer months.

All this has happened since the war and in the teeth of official apathy. And what is heroic and encouraging about the story is the way voluntary labour and voluntary subscriptions have made it possible. Mr Rolt himself was General Manager of the line until he could no longer afford to occupy that enjoyable but unremunerative post. The Talyllyn has been formed as a non-profit-making company. Railway enthusiasts young and old, Welsh and English, have worked on the line, most of them for nothing and in their holidays. To-day among those last pages of Bradshaw where the few independent railways left in these islands are listed, you may find once again the time-table of the Talyllyn. That insertion is the result of the independent spirit which still survives in this country and refuses to be crushed by the money-worshippers, centralisers and unimaginative theorists who are doing their best to kill it.

The particular appeal of this book will be to railway enthusiasts. The engines and rolling-stock, even the newer engines which have been acquired, have great historic interest. The scenery along the line, the bridges, the streams, the little stations, the tickets, the livery of the Company, have a more general appeal to all who love railways. The encouragement given by the public who travel on the line is a further testament to the growing popularity of a gentle journey on a small line, from which the country is so much more easily seen than from a motor car or bus. While those levellers, the clerks of the British Railways, are shutting down all the beautiful little country branch lines instead of devising a practical means of keeping them open, while they are killing the independent pride of the companies, while they are doing away with individual liveries and stamping their same ugly emblem on every engine, while they are concentrating only on express trains and selling the pass to the uncomfortable, unaccommodating, dangerous and hideous bus companies, the Talyllyn Railway is a working witness of the new revolution. Had the Talyllyn been included in 'British Railways', this experiment could never had been made. We 'own' British Railways, but we are allowed no say in them. We really do own the Talyllyn Railway. Perhaps its example will put life into the dead hand of British Railways and help to save our remaining branch lines. This book should certainly be an encouragement to such independent undertakings as the Ravenglass and Eskdale Railway, the South Shields, Marsden and Whitburn Colliery, the Snowdon Mountain, the Isle of Man Railways, the Sligo, Leitrim and Northern Counties, the County Donegal Joint, the Mumbles, the Mersey, the Liverpool Overhead and the Glasgow Underground, though the last four can probably carry on without voluntary support.

26th June, 1953

JOHN BETJEMAN

Chapter One

The setting of this adventure is a part of the ancient Welsh kingdom of Gwynedd, a land of mountains bounded on the north and south by the estuaries of the Mawddach and the Dovey and on the west by the shores of Cardigan Bay. The central keep of this region is Cader Idris whose storm-bitten peak of naked rock commands the coast of Wales from Bardsey Island to St David's Head and wave beyond wave of mountains from Snowdon to Aran Mawddwy and Plynlimon Fawr. Like three extended fingers of a hand, its outliers point westwards to the sea, enclosing between their narrow, knuckled ridges two deep and secluded valleys. Long ago the broader and more northerly of the two, the Dyffryn Dysynni, was an estuary like its neighbours the Mawddach and the Dovey, but where once there were shallow seas and shifting sand-banks the encircling heights now look down upon a quilt of green marshland seamed by the shining threads of drainage dykes. Craig-yr-Aderyn, the Bird Rock, dominates this marsh, a seven hundred foot face of almost sheer rock thrusting out into its levels like the prow of some hugh stranded ship. About the foot of this sea-forgotten cliff the white marsh mists swirl and dissolve soundlessly, thin ghosts of tides which only the sea birds hold in ancestral memory. For still they come to nest upon its inaccessible ledges, and about and above its stony face they wheel and cry perpetually.

The second valley bears no name upon the map. It is a deep and narrow defile, in places no broader than a single English meadow. The same river, the Dysynni, flows through the upper part of this valley, but geological chance has diverted it northwards from what would otherwise have been a direct course to the sea. No river has a more dramatic source than this Dysynni. For it spills out of Llyn Cae, a small pool, cold and still, whose deep waters, aquamarine in sunlight or dark as midnight in shadow, are the lees in the bottom of a mighty bowl of rock under the crest of Cader Idris. So like the crater of an extinct volcano is this savage amphitheatre of scree and precipice that it is easy to imagine a fiery torrent of molten rock flowing where now the young river plunges in cascade and thunderous fall down to the valley a thousand feet below. Here two dams formed by the landfalls of glacial erosion barred the Dysynni's passage seawards. Meeting the first, its waters spread to form the lake of Talyllyn before they forced a passage. The second obstruction, three miles below the lake at what is now the village of Abergynolwyn, was a much more formidable barrier. It diverted the river northwards through a narrow gorge into the present Dyffryn Dysynni, leaving the glacial valley immediately west of the obstruction as waterless as those in the English downland chalk. But soon small streams, falling headlong down the steep slopes, unite and fall asleep in the Afon Fathew, a lazy, wayward brook, undersized and obviously lost in so impressive a setting. It meanders under alders, through miniature marshes where black cattle ruminate and ranks of rushes fly yellow flags in late June, until it eventually loses itself in the Dysynni saltings.

In the flat lands between the junction of these two valleys and the sea stands the small town of Towyn, originally a group of unpretentious cottages of dark stone clustered about the ancient parish church of St Cadvan. All that now remains of the Dysynni estuary is an almost land-locked salt lake called the Broadwater a little to the north of the town. Yet there was a time when Towyn built and launched small sailing ships into the estuary and sent them away loaded with peat cut from the bogs of Craig Fach Goch which overlooks the town. But that maritime tradition has long ago been lost and forgotten. In the nineteenth century Towyn turned its back upon its silted, shrinking estuary and began to creep seawards in an effort to become a seaside resort. Thus it was that when the insatiable demands of the growing industrial cities of England led to the development of slate quarrying in the district, it was not to Towyn but to the neighbouring harbour of Aberdovey that the product of the new trade flowed.

TALYLLYN RAILWAY

SCALE OF MILES

ABERGYNOLWYN

BRYN EGLWYS

TO MACHYNLLETH

TO LLANFIHANGEL

TO TALYLLYN LAKE

STN:

1127

QUARRY

QUARRY SIDING

1613

1393

2076

TAREN HENDRE

DOLGOCH

NANT GWERNAL

CRAIG YR ADERYN
(BIRD ROCK)

FOEL WYLLT

AFON FATHEW

T.R.

FALLS

NANT DOLGOCH

TRUM GWR DOLGOCH

BRYNGLAS

PANDY

TYNYLLWYN HALT
1677

RHYDYRONEN

1806

TEREN CWM FFRNOL

TRUM GELLI

1743

NANT BRAICH-Y-RHIW

BRYN DINAS

PANT-YR-ON

LLYN BARFOG
(BEARDED LAKE)

CWM DYFFRYN

CYNFAL HALT

FACH-GOCH HALT

HENDY HALT

BRYNLLSG

PENDRE STN:

WHARF STN:

TOWYN

B.R. (W.R.)

RHOWNIAR

(HAPPY VALLEY)

A.493

ABERDOVEY

RIVER DOVEY

AFON DYFI

A.493

PENNAL

DOVEY JUNCTION

GLAN-DYFI

A.487

FOOTPATHS SHEWN THUS ----
SITE OF FORMER ----
MINERAL EXTENSION ++++

R.W.T.

LLANGELYNIN

LLANEGRYN

DYSYNNI

AFON DYSYNNI

DOLAUGWYN

BRYNCRUG

AFON DYFFRYN

A.493

TALY BONT

BEACON HILL

TONFANAU

AFON GWYLLT

BROAD WATER

MORFA GWYLLT

CARDIGAN BAY

TO BARMOUTH

M.A. Howard

KEY MAP

BARMOUTH
DOLGELLEY
TALYLLYN LAKE
TALYLLYN RLY.
ABERGYNOLWYN
MACHYNLLETH
TOWYN
DOVEY JUNCTION
ABERDOVEY
ABERYSTWYTH

Talyllyn Railway

'The line stops short three miles from Talyllyn'. General view looking towards the lake from which the railway takes its name

J.J. Davis

View of Wharf station with slate awaiting transhipment

F. Moores Railway Photographs, Talyllyn Railway Archive

That the Dovey valley is a geological boundary of importance the texture and contour of the mountains to north and south of it clearly reveal. Cader Idris and its lowlier neighbours are mountains typical of North Wales, uplifted masses of slate and felspathic trap whose higher and more acute foldings have been etched by wind and weather into a skyline of dark crests of jagged rock. South of the Dovey the mountains, even their king Plynlimon Fawr, are of smoother, kindlier shape, and except for occasional veins of lead they have offered few prizes for man to rifle. Here are none of the galleried precipices like gigantic steps, the caverns or monstrous tips by which man in his pursuit of slate has made his own contribution to the sombre and often forbidding grandeur of the North Wales mountain landscape.

The quarrying of the slate beds hereabouts was never prosecuted upon so great a scale as at Blaenau Festiniog, Llanberis or Penrhyn to the North, but one does not have to proceed far from the north bank of the Dovey before meeting evidence of extensive quarrying. The tips of the old quarries at Dinas Mawddwy almost spill into the waters of that river, while the narrow valley of its tributary the Afon Dulas is lined with workings, a few still operating but more derelict, from Esgair Geilog through Corris to Aberllefenni and remote Ratgoed. Many of these quarries are familiar by sight if not by name to the motorists who, in the holiday season, travel the main roads which wind through these valleys. But only a few of those who journey on foot into the mountains ever see the quarry of Bryn Eglwys ('The church on the hill') which is the particular concern of this story. Indeed, if slate had never been quarried at Bryn Eglwys there would have been no story to tell.

The quarry is perched upon a high plateau far from any metalled road and quite invisible from the valley below. Its grey buildings, workings and waste tips have made an impudent but puny scar upon a secret and otherwise inviolate solitude between the breasts of two peaks, Taren Hendre and Taren-y-Gesail, both over 2,000 feet high. From the quarry a track, as steep as it is rough, descends the flank of the densely wooded ravine of the Nant Gwernol to Abergynolwyn. Here the track joins the valley road and the

Gwernol flows into the Dysynni at the point where that river turns aside into the gorge that leads from the one valley to the other.

When John Pughe first began quarrying at Bryn Eglwys in 1847 the slates were carried by pack horses through the mountains to Aberdovey for shipment. This laborious and costly method of transport seriously restricted the development of the quarry and it is not surprising that before long the owners should have looked northwards to Portmadoc where a similar transport problem had already been solved. There, in 1836, after three years' work, an engineer named James Spooner had built a tramway fourteen miles long to connect that seaport with the quarries of Blaenau Festiniog in the Moelwyn mountains. With such skill had Spooner surveyed his route through this difficult country that loaded slate trains could be run by gravity practically the whole way from the quarries to Portmadoc, and horses were only required to haul back the empty trains. In 1863, soon after James Spooner's death, his younger son Charles introduced steam locomotives to take the place of these horses, although contemporary engineering opinion held that on a gauge so small as 1 ft. $11\frac{1}{2}$ ins. they would prove quite impracticable. But Charles Spooner confounded these critics. His experiment proved a brilliant success and the tramway soon became the Festiniog Railway, the first narrow gauge steam railway in the world. Profiting by this example the McConnel family, who were now the owners of Bryn Eglwys, proposed building a similar railway from their quarry to Aberdovey and appointed as their engineer Charles's elder brother, James Swinton Spooner. Before they reached the stage of seeking parliamentary powers, however, the promotion of the Aberystwyth and Welsh Coast Railway caused them to abandon the proposed line from Towyn to Aberdovey and to limit construction to six and a half miles of line from Abergynolwyn to the Coast Railway at the former place.

Because the mountain groups of southern Merioneth are of altogether simpler pattern than are those in the north, James Spooner was not confronted by any difficulties comparable with those which his father had faced when surveying his route between Portmadoc and Blaenau. He was able to project a line of railway on a practically straight course which climbed gradually upwards from Towyn along the southern slopes of the valley of the Afon Fathew as far as Abergynolwyn. The only major obstacle was the deep but narrow gorge of the tributary Dolgoch which Spooner planned to surmount by means of a viaduct of three spans. His Plans and Sections were submitted to the Parliamentary Session of 1865 and in that same year construction was authorised. The Talyllyn Railway Company had been born. Why the railway was ever given such a title has never been quite clear since the line stops short three miles from Talyllyn and there is no record of any proposal to carry it further at that time, nor would there have been any motive in so doing.

The plans submitted to Parliament show the railway terminating at the point half a mile west of Abergynolwyn where the valley is partially blocked by the landfall which diverted the Dysynni. The section from this point eastwards to the quarries of Bryn Eglwys, which included two rope worked inclines, Alltwyllt and Cantrybedd, was the subject of a separate and subsequent plan which Spooner entitled 'Extension of Talyllyn Railway' and which was never submitted to Parliament. The reason for this, presumably, was that whereas the promoters intended from the outset to operate a public passenger service between Towyn and Abergynolwyn, the remaining section to the quarries, although a part of the Company's undertaking, was looked upon as a private mineral extension. One stipulation in the authorising Act was that the railway might be built to any gauge provided it was not more than 4 ft. $8\frac{1}{2}$ ins. or less than 2 ft. 3 ins. At a time when the 'Battle of the Gauges' between the supporters of Brunel and Stephenson had provided a recent object lesson in the disadvantages of non-standard gauges, it seems curious that the Talyllyn Railway should have been specifically prevented by this clause from adopting the Festiniog gauge of 1 ft. $11\frac{1}{2}$ ins. which had already proved so successful further north. However, the decision to construct the line to the gauge of 2 ft. 3 ins. may have been influenced by the fact that a horse tramway of this gauge was already operating in the neighbouring Corris valley. In view of the proximity of Bryn Eglwys to the Upper Corris quarries it may even be that trams of this gauge were in use in and around the workings at Bryn Eglwys before the railway was built. If this was the case the choice of gauge may have been determined by a local precedent already esablished.

The line from Towyn to Abergynolwyn is described on the Deposited Plans as 'Line No. 1'. 'Line No. 2' was a short extension which, by means of a spur and a reversal, would have given the narrow gauge direct access to the main line station at Towyn. But although construction of this 'Line No. 2' was authorised by the Act, for some reason unknown the powers were never exercised.

When we contrast the time which elapses to-day between the plan and the execution of any construction scheme with the speed with which the Victorians went to work without any of our bulldozers, excavators or other elaborate mechanical aids, it is difficult to resist the melancholy conclusion that our civilisation must be losing its vitality and sinking into slow decline like an old man in his dotage. Admittedly the Talyllyn Railway was not a work of great magnitude, but when we find Managing Director McConnel requesting formal inspection of the works by the Board of Trade in the early autumn of 1866, we realise that the little Company had certainly wasted no time. Nor had the firms who supplied the necessary equipment and rolling stock, notably Messrs Fletcher, Jennings & Co. of Lowca Works, Whitehaven, Cumberland, who had built two locomotives to the Company's order.

The first of these engines, No. 1 TALYLLYN, was delivered in the autumn of 1865 while the railway was still under construction and was one of the first major consignments to arrive at Towyn over Thomas Savin's newly opened Aberystwyth & Welsh Coast Railway. TALYLLYN was a four coupled saddle tank locomotive of orthodox contemporary design except for her slim gauge. But her sister engine, No. 2 DOLGOCH, which joined her a year later, was by no means so conventional, and her maker's plate proudly proclaimed that she was 'Fletcher's Patent'. She was of 0–4–0 wheel arrangement like No. 1, but here the resemblance ceased for

THE LOWCA ENGINEERING COMPANY, LIMITED,

Lowca Engine Works, Whitehaven, England.

CLASS Bb.

FLETCHER'S "PATENT" TANK LOCOMOTIVE ENGINE FOR NARROW GAUGES.

THIS Engine is designed for use where the curves are easy, and a long wheel base is in consequence admissible, securing greater steadiness than can be obtained with Engines in which the wheel base is short and the firebox overhangs the driving axle.

The Cylinders are placed outside, and the driving axle is situated behind the firebox instead of before it. The eccentrics which give motion to the slide valves are put upon the leading or front axle instead of the driving one, and a peculiar arrangement of link motion employed.

One of these Engines, with 8-inch cylinders, has been some years at work on a railway, 2ft. 3in. gauge, in North Wales, for the conveyance of minerals and passengers. Up gradients of 1 in 75 and 1 in 66 (the latter half a mile long) its usual load is 33 tons, at a speed of 18 miles an hour.

Dimensions and Prices for Gauges under 3½ft.

Code Word.	Size of Cylinder.	Length of Stroke.	Area of Firegrate.	No. of Tubes.	Diameter of Tubes.	Size of Wheels.	Wheel Centres.	Size of Injector.	Diameter of Boiler.	Length of Boiler Barrel.	Gauge of Rails.	Ap'roxim'te Weight when Empty.	Nett Cash Price.
	In.	In.	Ft.		In.	Ft. In.	Ft. In.	No.	Ft. In.	Ft. In.	Ft. In.	Tons.	
BENBOW	8	16	4	73	1½	2 6	6 6	4	2 6¾	4 9	2 3 to 3 6	8½	£650
BARBEL	9	16	4¾	78	1½	2 9	7 0	4	2 9	5 3	3 0 to 3 6	9½	£760
BULBUL	10	20	6	110	1½	3 0	8 0	5	3 0	6 0		11	£860

'To a small Welsh town of 1865, a steam locomotive must have seemed as new fangled and as mysterious a machine as a jet aircraft would be to-day.' The picture shows a contemporary catalogue design

Talyllyn Railway Archive

No. 1 at Aber, whose 'vertical motion' had so alarmed Captain Tyler in 1866

No. 2 locomotive when named PRETORIA whose 'horizontal oscillation' complained of in the same Board of Trade Report may have remained unaltered until the Society took over

photographs: Talyllyn Railway Archive

she had an abnormally long rigid wheel-base of 6 ft. 6 ins., the rear (driving) axle being situated behind the firebox and immediately in front of the water tank which was mounted at the back of the footplate. The maker's objective was a four coupled locomotive with all weight available for adhesion and without any excessive overhang at front or rear. This was achieved, but at a price. So long a rigid wheel-base proved punishing to the lightly laid permanent way, while to incorporate the inside valve motion, which was almost universally favoured at that time, a devious and not altogether satisfactory expedient had to be adopted. Because the rear driving axle was behind the firebox, the eccentrics must needs be mounted on the leading axle whence they drove the Allan straight link motion, while the valve rods, of banjo form to clear the axle, passed between these eccentrics. This means that the valves were driven via the coupling rods, and the more technically minded will appreciate that this added source of lost motion gravely prejudiced the maintenance of an accurate valve setting. Moreover, sandwiched between such narrow frames, the lay-out was necessarily cramped and inaccessible.

When they were delivered, neither locomotive possessed a cab or even a weather board, a disregard for the comfort of their crews and for the vagaries of the Welsh mountain climate which was typical of those hardy days. Cabs were built later on both engines.

To a small Welsh town of 1865, a steam locomotive must have seemed as new fangled and as mysterious a machine as a jet aircraft would be to-day. Imagine a 'Comet' airliner being delivered for the use of some remote village without pilot or ground crew and you have a situation not dissimilar from that created at Towyn by the arrival of 'TALYLLYN'. A local man was found who claimed to have had some experience with a portable farm engine, but his efforts to coax the locomotive into life were by all accounts as unsuccessful as would be an attempt by the village garage mechanic to induce the 'Comet' to become airborne. Finally, in response to a desperate appeal from the Company for assistance, Messrs Fletcher, Jennings sent down one of their fitters by the name of Bousted. This expert of the new age of steam proceeded to set the engine to work with such efficiency and despatch that he was invited to take permanent charge of the locomotive department. After some discussion he agreed and moved his wife and family from Cumberland to Abergynolwyn where the engine shed was at first situated. Later, a cottage was built for him adjoining the new shed and repair shop at Towyn, and here Bousted remained until he emigrated to Australia eighteen years later.

We may assume that the commencement of slate traffic on the railway coincided with Bousted's arrival, but before the railway could be opened for public passenger services the approval of the Board of Trade was necessary. As a result of McConnel's application, the Board instructed Captain H.W. Tyler to carry out a formal inspection of the railway on September 8th, 1866. His report, written from Aberystwyth on the 25th of that month, is quite a lengthy document but is worth quoting in full for its historical interest and for the description of the railway as first constructed.

Aberystwyth,
25th September, 1866.

Sir,

I have the honour to report for the information of the Lords of the Committee of Privy Council for Trade, that in compliance with the instructions contained in your minute of the 8th instant I have inspected the Talyllyn Railway.

This is a single line 6 miles and 50.75 chains long, constructed on a gauge of 2 ft. 3 ins. between the rails. The steepest gradient is 1 in 60. The sharpest curve has a radius of 6 chains. There are only two stations, namely Towyn at one end and Abergynolwyn at the other.

The permanent way is laid with rails of the I [flat-bottomed] section weighing 44 lbs. per lineal yard, and in lengths of 21 ft. There are cast iron chairs weighing $20\frac{1}{2}$ lbs. each at the joints of the rails, and $17\frac{1}{4}$ lbs. each for two intermediate chairs under each side. The sleepers are laid transversely 3 feet apart and are stated to average 4 ft. 9 ins. long by 7 ins. by 5 ins. The chairs are secured to the sleepers by iron spikes, and the intermediate portions of the rails between the chairs by dog spikes. I recommend that locked chock blocks be added to the sidings and duplicate connecting rods to the switches.

The fences are principally of post and rail with five rails, and in some places of hedges. They require raising or improvement and the hedges to be repaired, in some places, as I have pointed out in going over the line.

There are 7 bridges over and 15 under the Railway, besides a viaduct 51 feet high, and 38 yards long. At a bridge $3\frac{1}{2}$ miles from Towyn the wall plate under the beams should be better secured and the beams should in this and other instances be bolted together towards each end. Two brick arches, one at $1\frac{1}{4}$ mile and the other at $\frac{3}{4}$ mile from Talyllyn [Towyn?] should be rebuilt.

The Bridges over the line have a span on the square of only 9 ft. 1 in. or 9 ft. $1\frac{1}{2}$ in. and the only passenger carriage which has yet been purchased is 5 ft. $3\frac{1}{2}$ in. wide outside measurement. This leaves but 1 ft. 11 ins. between the outside of the carriage and the abutments, instead of 2 ft. 6 ins. which there ought to be. Mr McConnel, the Chairman of the Company, proposes to obviate this difficulty by permanently fastening the door and barring the windows on one side of his carriages and slewing the rails so as to allow sufficient space between the other side and the abutment. The objection to his course is that if a carriage was turned over on the unbarred side, with the barred side uppermost, the passengers would be unable to escape from it. But it must be admitted that this objection has not the same force in the case of a line of this description, on which only one engine will be employed for passengers and minerals at a speed intended to be not greater than 10 miles an hour and on which the passenger traffic will be so limited that it would not be worth while for the Company to carry passengers at all if much extra expense was to be incurred in the works as on lines of higher speed and greater traffic. It is necessary that other carriages should be provided.

The Company has only two engines of which the heaviest is said to weigh 8 tons in working order – one of them is at work and the other under repair. It is desirable that some alteration should be made in them, with a view to check the vertical motion to which the one is liable from its short wheel base, and the horizontal oscillation which is caused with the other by the action of outside cylinders upon a crank pin of excessive length in proportion to the diameter of the driving wheels.

Pending the completion of the various improvements which I have indicated I am obliged to report my opinion that this little line cannot be opened by reason of the incompleteness of the works without danger to the Public using it.

I have, etc.,

(Sgd.) H.W. TYLER.

It is evident from this Report that anxiety to get the railway in full operation had resulted in too much haste and too little forethought. But the Company evidently lost no time in taking steps to remedy the matters of which Captain Tyler complained, for we find him making a second inspection a month later and reporting upon it from Aberdovey in November as follows:

Aberdovey,
8th November, 1866.

Sir,

I have the honour to report, for the information of the Lords of the Committee of Privy Council for Trade, that in compliance with the instructions contained in your minute of the 15th ulto: I have re-inspected the Talyllyn Railway.

I find that the fencing has been improved, the 3 Bridges to which I referred in my report of the 25th September last have been rebuilt, chock blocks have been added to the sidings, and indicators and duplicate connecting rods to the switches. I recommended that some gates which were being put up near the Towyn Station should be placed further from the rails.

There is still only one passenger carriage on the line, but another has been constructed and is on its way. Mr McConnel, the Chairman of the Company, informs me that he expects only 3 or 4 passengers for each train except on Saturdays, when he expects 30 or 40. It is desirable that extra carriages should be provided, before next spring.

The Engine which was working during my previous visit, is still at work, but with some slight alterations which have tended to make it more steady; and Mr McConnel informs me he has now determined to add trailing wheels to the other Engine as I have recommended. He will also shorten the crank pins on the driving wheels of the working Engine as soon as the other has been got ready to take its place. I travelled on the line to-day at a speed of 20 miles an hour with the working engine, and found it steadier than I expected at that speed, and Mr McConnel does not propose in the course of working to exceed 10 miles per hour.

The safety of the single line will be secured by the employment of only one engine at a time as provided for in the certificate of the 6th September.

Subject to the above conditions, and to the precautions referred to in my report of the 25th September in regard to narrow works, I am of opinion that this little line may be opened without danger to the public using it.

I have, etc.,

(Sgd.) H.W. TYLER.

These reports reveal several points of interest. First, the student of railways will note the curious construction of the permanent way which employed a flat-bottomed rail partly spiked to sleepers and partly held in chairs. As originally laid there were no fishplates connecting one rail to another. Instead the two rail ends rested in a common chair and were secured there by an oak key. This made a perfectly satisfactory joint, but one that called for a high standard of maintenance. For if the oak key fell out, or if one rail end dropped out of the chair owing to track creep, the two rails were no longer positively located laterally with results which could be highly dangerous. Although this disadvantage was not commented upon by Captain Tyler, it was evidently recognised by the Company who subsequently set two men to work to drill every rail end with a hand operated ratchet drill and to fit fishplates. As each joint of the two rails involved drilling eight holes, the length of the line was six and a half miles and the rails were 21 ft. long, those with a weakness for statistics can work out for themselves what this job involved. Starting at Towyn and working their way up the valley, it kept the two men busy for some years, but though it provided a steady job it must have been a monotonous one, and it is hardly surprising to find that an occasional joint was accidentally or deliberately missed. In addition, the last section of track up to Abergynolwyn remained in its original condition, though whether this indicates the ultimate discouragement, retirement or death of the two drillers is not known.

Another point of interest to be found in the second report is McConnel's astonishingly low estimate of potential passenger traffic. He may not have anticipated a great volume of tourist traffic at this early date, but the railway was then the only means of transport in the valley, and even to-day when the train has to compete with a bus service and the motor car, local passengers alone still frequently exceed the 'three or four' of McConnel's estimate. If he seriously rated the traffic so low the surprising thing is that the Company should have contemplated working a public service at all in view of the formalities and the additional safety precautions which this involved. It seems much more likely that McConnel deliberately played down the railway's passenger carrying potential with the object of encouraging Captain Tyler to take a more tolerant view of the working arrangements! To judge from the tone of the report, this happy result was duly achieved.

The single coach mentioned in the reports was supplied by the Lancaster Wagon Works, a firm which may have been recommended to the Company by Messrs Fletcher, Jennings. The additional vehicle described as being 'on its way' was actually one of three almost identical coaches which were built for the railway by the firm of Brown, Marshall of Birmingham. Like their predecessor they were three compartment four-wheelers but of a more modern design and appearance. The arrival of a four-wheeled brake-van completed the catalogue of passenger rolling-stock. Unlike the three coaches, this last no longer carries a maker's nameplate, but identical details of construction make it obvious that it was also supplied by Marshalls. We shall have occasion to examine this rolling-stock more closely in a later chapter.

The good Captain's strictures on the two locomotives raise some interesting speculations, but whatever faults these engines may have possessed, in fairness to their builders it must not be forgotten that they were among the earliest small gauge machines ever built. Reference to a short wheel-base makes it clear that the engine whose 'vertical motion' alarmed Captain Tyler was No. 1 TALYLLYN. If we look at this engine to-day and imagine her without trailing wheels, even the least mechanically minded will appreciate that her behaviour may well have given every cause for alarm. McConnel fulfilled his undertaking to Captain Tyler by having No. 1 fitted with trailing wheels. I conjecture that in this process the existing frames were modified at the rear and that this alteration was not lastingly satisfactory. Frame weakness was in any case a fault of both engines. For I have it on the authority of an old driver that TALYLLYN was subsequently rebuilt at Towyn in a new frame which was supplied by Bagnalls of Stafford. As will appear later, there is concrete evidence to support this, otherwise I should have doubted whether such a major operation could have been carried out on the spot.

The Captain's criticism of No. 2 DOLGOCH and McConnel's proposed method of overcoming it is much more mysterious. The point of the criticism is clear enough, but it is scarcely credible that the crank pins could ever have been shortened, as any locomotive engineer will appreciate, without radically altering the engine design. I suspect that once Captain Tyler was safely out of the way, this particular good intention was quietly forgotten and that to-day, after eighty-six years, DOLGOCH remains just as susceptible to 'horizontal oscillation' as ever she was.

Having received the blessing of the 'Lords of the Committee of Privy Council for Trade' the Company were at liberty to inaugurate their passenger service and this they proceeded to do without delay in December, 1866. No copy of the Company's first time-table seems to have survived, but according to local press reports there were two trains a day each way, leaving Abergynolwyn at 8 a.m. and 3 p.m. and returning from Towyn Pendre at 9 a.m. and 4 p.m., the journey time being forty minutes. The earliest extant time-table is dated February 19th, 1867, and is reproduced here. The reason for the introduction of a completely revised time-table so soon and at such an arbitrary date was most probably that the new locomotive shed at Towyn Pendre had been completed and was brought into use for the first time on this February day in 1867. For whereas the earliest daily services had originated and terminated at Abergynolwyn, the point of origin now and for ever after is Towyn. It will also be noticed on this 1867 time-table that since Captain Tyler's visit an intermediate station had been opened at Rhydyronen. Two more stations were built subsequently at Brynglas and Dolgoch higher up the valley, while several semi-official halting places at farm crossings became sanctioned by time and custom, one of them, at Cynfal, eventually boasting a diminutive platform. From the point of view of local traffic, Rhydyronen was, and for that matter still is, the most important intermediate station. At one time it even boasted a loop siding to handle the output of a small slate quarry situated nearby in the valley of the Nant Braich-y-Rhiw, a tributary of the Afon Fathew. But after a fatal rock fall this quarry closed down and the points at the western end of the loop were taken out to make the siding a dead end which was sufficient for ordinary local goods traffic. A similar dead-end siding was laid in at Brynglas, a station which was opened to serve the needs of the three farms and the old woollen mill with its attendant cottages which form the hamlet of Pandy. Dolgoch alone has never possessed a siding or even road access and it seems clear that it was built with an eye to tourist traffic rather than to meet a local demand.

The King's Station at Towyn referred to in the 1867 time-table was the terminus of the railway and the point of slate transhipment to standard gauge metals. It was so called after a previous owner of the property on which it stands, and not to commemorate any royal visit, for the railway has never been thus honoured in all its long life. Despite the fact that King's Station would have been very much more convenient for passengers changing to or from the Coast Railway, throughout McConnel's régime all Talyllyn passenger trains terminated and began their journeys at Pendre at the opposite end of the town from the main line station. This inconvenience was for a time mitigated to some extent by the employment of a donkey, which was stabled at Pendre, to carry passengers' luggage between the two stations, but it must have had an adverse effect on the development of tourist traffic. Evidently the slate traffic was of sufficient volume and importance to make the convenience of passengers a second- ary consideration, and it was not until after the control of the railway passed into other hands in 1911 that a passenger booking office was opened at King's and we find the terminus appearing in the time-tables and in Bradshaw for the first time under the name of the Wharf Station. Even so, certain trains continued to stop short at Pendre including those run for quarrymen. With the extension of services to the Wharf, overall journey time was increased from forty to forty-five minutes. No platform or other passenger facilities were provided at the Wharf, and as there was no run-round loop the passenger stock had to be propelled to and from the loop at Pendre.

The opening of the railway naturally led to considerable development in the quarry at Bryn Eglwys and to the employ- ment of more labour there. Abergynolwyn grew from a hamlet into a mining village, a microcosm of the industrial revolution isolated in the heart of this lonely Welsh valley. Its new rows of quarrymen's cottages looked as dark, as dour and as incapable of concession to their surroundings as those which were terracing the valleys of the Rhondda and the Ebbw. But this new crop could never flourish upon the slate as it did upon the coal measures. On the south side of the village two short terraces eye each other across an unmade road which begins and ends nowhere. It looks as though a section had been arbitrarily chopped out of a mean street in any industrial city and transplanted in the abortive hope that it might take root and grow.

To supply the needs of this community a new funicular was constructed by the railway Company from the level of the quarry extension down to the village 140 ft. below, its course being marked in pencil by a later hand on Spooner's plan of the extension. From the foot of this incline, lines were laid through the village to bring coal and other supplies to the very doors of many of the cottages. In recent years these lines have disappeared

15

so that there is now no overt evidence that the village is served at all by rail, and to the stranger entering Abergynolwyn from the east the sign of 'The Railway Hotel' on the only public house must appear to be a curious misnomer.

To reach the quarries from the village involved a climb of 700 ft. in little over a mile so it is hardly surprising that the quarrymen rode the wagons on the inclines if they could in spite of the danger and the fact that the practice was officially frowned upon. Wagons were drawn up on a wire cable by means of their descending fellows and speed could be controlled to some extent by a crude hand-brake on the cable drum at the top of each incline. But 'break-aways' were by no means infrequent, the wagons usually terminating explosively in the bottom of the Nant Gwernol ravine. One quarryman who was riding in a wagon which broke away would certainly never have lived to tell the tale had he not been catapulted into the upper branches of a tree to hang there almost unhurt but terrified out of his wits as the wagon was smashed to pieces on the rocks below.

By no means all the labour in the quarry was drawn from Abergynolwyn. Many came from further afield, and for their benefit a special train was introduced which left Towyn at six o'clock each Monday morning to take them to work. These men remained up at Bryn Eglwys all the week, sleeping and eating in a primitive hostel called 'the barracks', and returning by another special train every Friday evening. The return workings of both these trains were used by children who tramped over the mountains from as far afield as Corris to travel to or from the school at Towyn where they boarded during the week.

As the passenger rolling-stock possessed no form of heating or lighting, travel by those early morning and evening trains in the depth of winter must have been as frigid as it was gloomy. The unfortunate quarrymen, sitting on the unyielding seats in stygian darkness could not even enjoy the solace of a pipe of shag, for the Regulations of the Company empowered the Guard to eject from the train anyone so depraved as to indulge in this horrid vice. These same Regulations also threatened passengers with dire penalties if they attempted to ride on the roofs of the coaches, while the Staff Rules forbade the Guard to walk thereon. It is highly unlikely that this edict was ever invoked in the history of the Company since it is inconceivable that anyone in his senses would occupy so perilous a perch from choice, particularly in the early hours of a cold winter's morning.

The most serious mishap in the history of the Company befell one of these early morning quarrymen's trains. At a place now known as Quarry Siding between Dolgoch and Abergynolwyn in the faint half-light of a winter dawn the train crew failed to see that torrential rain on the preceding Sunday had blocked the line with a heap of silt and gravel washed down from the mountain. On hitting this obstruction the train left the rails and proceeded for some distance down the steep mountain track which crosses the line at this point before it finally came to rest with one coach lying on its side. Happily no one was seriously hurt, nor did the train apparently sustain much damage, and with the aid of a strong muster of labour from the quarry it was righted and dragged back to its track. As a result of this alarming incident it became the custom for the old Irishman who was foreman platelayer in those days to run ahead of the Monday morning train on a self-propelled trolley to ensure that neither Act of God nor human mischief had obstructed the line during the preceding week-end.

With this exception the history of the little railway was marked by few dramatic events. There was the occasional minor derailment, while more than one incautious mountain sheep met a gory end on the track, its carcass usually disappearing without trace into the firebox. Sometimes there came a winter blizzard to whip the snow off the steep mountain sides and bury the narrow track. Railway and quarry workers alike would then set to work to dig their way through the drifts so that much needed coal and stores could be brought up to Abergynolwyn and slate stocks released from snowbound Bryn Eglwys. But in this western valley, so much more remote then than it is to-day, the uneventful years slipped gently by with little to record their passing but the recurring patterns of the changing seasons; the colour of the mountains changing from the brown of the curled bracken frond to the heavy green of high summer and the bronze of autumn; the human activity in the valleys below following its own ordered sequence of seed-time, haysel and harvest, of lambing time and wool clip. In this small, tranquil world bounded by sea and mountain, where the great waves of change and conflict in Europe beat with no more effect than the ripples on a mill pond, the two little locomotives of the Talyllyn Railway clanked their imperturbable way through the most momentous and distracted years in human history. To this day there are old men in the valley who speak of the railway's coming as though it were yesterday, and there is one nonagenarian who remembers the line being built. That one lifetime should have bridged so wide a gulf seems scarcely credible, for when we look back at the world into which the railway was born, it seems to have become as remote as the Middle Ages. For in 1865 the reign of Victoria was at its zenith of prosperity and self-confidence, and except for a few far-sighted men like John Ruskin, the misery and squalor in the new industrial cities was regarded, if it was regarded at all, as but a transient phase in the automatic progress of man towards a millennium of peace and prosperity. In the world of politics Disraeli had not yet become Prime Minister; in literature Charles Dickens had just published *Our Mutual Friend* while Tennyson was at the height of his powers and had still to complete his *Idylls of the King*; on the stage, a promising young man named Henry Irving was attracting favourable notice in the part of Hamlet. It was the age of the crinoline, of gaslight and of the hansom cab. Although Faraday was nearing the end of his life and the first gas engine had been patented, electric power and the internal combustion engine were still to come. Indeed, Henry Royce, who was destined to bestow his name upon the finest motor car in the world, was a two-year-old infant. Even the great age of steam had still to reach its zenith. Patrick Stirling's first 8 ft. single-driver had not left the drawing board at Doncaster, and the days of superheated steam, of the Westinghouse and vacuum brake had not dawned; Isambard Brunel was but lately dead and the Great Western Railway still owned fifteen hundred miles of 7 ft. gauge track.

But turn now from this picture to that of the first years of the new century. The long high summer of the Victorian Age is over and it is the Edwardian evening, a golden evening yet one in which many now realised that summer could not last for ever. Already the clouds of the Boer War temporarily darkened the sky as a portent of the night that was so soon to fall over all Europe. Even in Merioneth these clouds, appearing in skies which for so long had been cloudless, evidently did not pass entirely unnoticed, for with patriotic zeal the name of the second Talyllyn locomotive was temporarily changed from DOLGOCH to PRETORIA. But no portents affected the pace of the technical revolution. Electric light and the telephone were now no longer scientific novelties, and the motor car, soon outgrowing its first stuttering efforts in the 'nineties, was beginning to master the English roads and even to brave the hills of Wales. On the railways the Broad Gauge had become a memory and already Patrick Stirling's 8 ft. single was an obsolete type. For Churchward was building six-coupled express locomotives at Swindon, and corridor express trains, little different from those we know, were roaring along the main lines to schedules which were often faster than those which prevail to-day. Yet no symptoms of these forty years of rapid engineering and scientific progress were manifest on the Talyllyn Railway. Drawn by the same two locomotives the same train of hard-seated four-wheelers rattled up and down the valley, still without any form of lighting or any such new-fangled device as continuous brakes.

Owing to a vagary of industrial history, these were the most prosperous years of the quarry at Bryn Eglwys and consequently the railway carried its heaviest slate traffic at this time. Further north at Penrhyn the quarrymen began an unsuccessful strike which lasted for five years. During all this time, while bands of quarrymen travelled about the country singing for a living, the great slate quarry, whose proud boast it was to be the largest in the world, lay silent and deserted. So large had been its output that its closure created an acute demand for slate which, almost over-night, caused a boom in the smaller quarries such as Bryn Eglwys. Like other Welsh quarry owners, W.H. McConnel, son of the railway's first chairman, was quick to exploit the shortage, and in those five years he reaped a small fortune. Yet the results of the

19

Penrhyn strike proved disastrous and dealt a blow to the Welsh slate industry from which it never recovered. For the output of Penrhyn had been such that even the combined get-rich-quick efforts of the rest of the industry could not completely satisfy the demands of the building trade which consequently began to look elsewhere for roofing material. The production of machine-made tiles was stimulated and for the first time in history foreign slates were imported to England from Italy and elsewhere. These imported slates were inferior in quality to the Welsh product, but they were cheaper and the foreigner has never lost the market since. Moreover, some Welsh owners seem to have been concerned only to take advantage of this brief boom by extracting the maximum slate in the minimum of time to the neglect of capital development and with results disastrous to the future of their quarries. This, unfortunately, was the story of Bryn Eglwys. In 1911, not long after the Penrhyn strike was over, McConnel pocketed his profits and sold both Bryn Eglwys and his controlling interest in the Talyllyn Railway Company to Sir Henry Haydn Jones, a local worthy and the Member of Parliament for the County of Merioneth.

Sir Haydn acquired a dubious bundle of assets. There was, it is true, no lack of good slate in the mountain at Bryn Eglwys, but in order to work it, and work it efficiently, fresh underground development and new plant was urgently needed. Existing levels had either been worked out or their subterranean chambers were in a highly dangerous condition owing to the lack of sufficient roof support. Only the knowledge of the hardship in the district which closure of the quarry would cause persuaded the local Inspector of Mines to allow work to continue as the lesser of two evils. In these dark bowels of the mountain even the small sound of water dripping became charged with a significance as sinister as the tick of a time bomb. Percolating through faults in the roof overhead it was often the only warning of the sudden thunderous fall of hundreds of tons of rock. And it was under these conditions that men, armed with crowbars, swung like human battering rams on ropes suspended from above to dislodge from the working face the slabs that previous shots had loosened. There might be no danger of fire or explosion, but one old quarryman who migrated to the South Wales pits assured me that the hazards of deep coal mining were nothing to him after his experience in the treacherous caverns of Bryn Eglwys. The only major change in quarrying methods since the nineteenth century was the installation of two air compressors driven by water-wheels which supplied air power to the working face. This was not popular with the men. Apart from their deafening noise, the pneumatic drills brought with them to the face the dread of silicosis from slate dust which had always haunted the cutting sheds, where no attempt was ever made to extract the deadly dust set up by the slate saws.

In this matter of equipment the quarry undoubtedly suffered from the inaccessibility of its lofty and lonely situation, and as much maintenance work as possible was done in the repair shop on the spot, even down to the casting of bearing brasses. It is surprising how some of the heavier machinery was ever got up to the quarry, for everything had to be drawn up the vertiginous gradients of the Alltwyllt and Cantrybedd inclines on the small narrow gauge wagons. Perhaps the most remarkable of these transport feats was performed one summer when an exceptional drought dried up the reservoir in the mountains above Bryn Eglwys whose waters, driving overshot and Pelton wheels, provided the quarry's only source of power. To prevent work from coming to a standstill, temporary steam plant was brought up and installed at short notice.

McConnel left the railway in little better case than the quarry and his successor, Sir Haydn Jones, never saw fit to expend the capital which both sorely needed. It is true that the railway had never shown a profit on paper, but it was the lifeline of the quarry and as both undertakings had always been under common owner-ship, for the railway to make a profit on its staple traffic would merely have been a question of book entry, of paying money out of one pocket into the other.

So through the cataclysm of the First World War and through the years of uneasy peace which followed, both quarry and railway continued in much the same way as they had done in the past. But the labour began to ebb way from the quarry, while on the railway it became more than ever a case of 'make do and mend' as a steadily deteriorating permanent way began to rack the life out of the ageing locomotives and rolling-stock. But during the summer seasons a new class of traffic, which old Mr McConnel had scarcely dreamed of when he launched the Talyllyn Railway Company, was doing something to offset the declining slate trade. Every summer improving transport brought more and more people into Wales from the growing industrial areas of the Midlands and South Lancashire. Over the ruins of the old local industries which these same industrial areas had helped to destroy, the Welsh tourist trade grew up. Like many another small township in Wales, Towyn began perforce to look beyond its mountains for a livelihood by catering for the annual invasion from England with results detrimental to its character and to its appearance. Boarding houses sprang up of that dour, grey and unwelcoming appearance peculiar to the smaller Welsh seaside resort which might have been deliberately designed to damp the holiday spirit. In this particular instance, as we have seen, old Towyn was not a seaside town at all, and the moving spirit of its transformation was William Corbett of Ynys Maengwyn. Corbett came of an established local family of considerable estate and standing, but it was in England that he amassed the fortune which enabled him to leave so notable a mark on his Welsh property. He industrialised the ancient salt trade of Droitwich with great profit to himself and ultimately disposed of his interest by striking an excellent bargain with that early cartel the Salt Union. His monument to these successful transactions in Droitwich consists of an immense replica in red brick of a French château which he built to make his French wife feel at home. In Towyn he built a large hotel, the 'Corbett Arms', whose many windows gaze boldly down the main street from a commanding site near the old church. More ambitious still, he constructed a promenade by the shore of Cardigan Bay. Where before there had been only sand dunes and marram grass there rose a massive sea wall which fronted a wind-swept platform of macadam almost broad enough for a barrack square. A marble tablet set in one end of the sea wall commemorates this achievement and its eminent author. To-day this grandiose front, bitten in places by the hungry sea, has the same truncated appearance and conveys the same impression of unfulfilled expectations as the short street of workmen's cottages in Abergynolwyn. For there are wide gaps like missing teeth in the cliff of boarding houses along its landward side, while at one end the spacious esplanade suddenly peters out and becomes a winding lane so narrow that two vehicles cannot pass. At its other, northern, end it is joined at right angles by what is virtually an extension of Towyn's long main street which has burrowed under the main railway and stretched itself seawards to meet this new amenity. But the buildings which line this seaward extension are patently of later date than Corbett's sea front, thus revealing that progress towards the union which justified the addition of the coveted words 'on-sea' to the name of this old market town proved painfully slow.

In the first years of the railway's history tourist traffic seems to have consisted mainly of annual outings by special train organised by the local chapel ministers for their flocks. Nowadays the aim of such outings seems to be to cover the greatest possible amount of ground in the day. Parties leave by coach at cock crow for their distant destination to return exhausted and fretful in the early hours of the following morning. But in those days they were less venturesome for some of the parties which entrained at Towyn travelled no further than Rhydyronen, two miles away. While the railway continued to cater for these modest local jamborees, we soon find the Company appealing to the summer occupants of Corbett's new Towyn-on-Sea. Time-tables and a small illustrated Guide Book which the Company published before the First World War reveal the contemporary Welsh realisation of the commercial possibilities of the 'picturesque'. The beauties of the Dolgoch ravine and its waterfalls were extolled, while the Company proclaimed that it possessed the cheapest and quickest route to Talyllyn Lake and Cader Idris regardless of the fact that these scenic splendours were over three miles beyond its Abergynolwyn railhead. Nevertheless, the statement was to some extent justifiable when the only alternative form of transport was a hired wagonette plodding along the narrow and dusty valley road or a journey from Machynlleth via the rival Corris Railway. But the same slogan continued to appear in bold type on the time-tables long after the coming of the motor bus had robbed it of the smallest claim to truth.

Even Rhydyronen was not overlooked in this early publicity campaign, for here visitors suffering from nervous debility were encouraged by the Guide Book to alight in order to imbibe the waters of a chalybeate spring at nearby Caerfynnon farm. For the benefit of potential patients a path was cut through the little wood where this spring is situated and the pipe through which the soothing waters flowed was embellished by a surround of white glazed brick of a kind we usually associate with a commoner and more mundane public amenity. At one time the waters were even made available in bottles bearing an elaborate label in the style of *art nouveau*. But alas for potential railway revenue, a remote mountain hamlet could never offer those facilities for polite social intercourse which were considered by our forbears to be as important a part of the fashionable pastime of 'taking the waters' as the waters themselves. So Rhydyronen has never featured in the list of British watering places and the Company never considered it worth their while to add the word 'Spa' to the station name-board.

Few passengers can have patronised the railway solely for health reasons; indeed, in its latter years such a journey would certainly have neutralised any beneficial effect which may have been derived from the waters so far as nervous disorders were concerned. But for those in search of the 'picturesque' the line had a strong appeal. Traffic grew steadily year by year and an estimate of its importance may be gathered from the proposal to construct an extension railway from Abergynolwyn via Talyllyn Lake to the Corris Railway at Upper Corris. This scheme was never more than a proposal. It would have involved a line costly to build and difficult to work, but that it was seriously advanced with an eye to tourist attraction alone is a measure of the value which had come to be attached to such traffic. In default of this extension, services of wagonettes plied between the Pen-y-Bont Hotel on Talyllyn Lake and Abergynolwyn and Corris stations respectively. By this

Gravity working: 'in connection with tourist traffic a practice far more fraught with possibilities of disaster became common during the holiday season'

'Terminating explosively in the Nant Gwernol ravine.' A slate wagon broken away from winding gear to the Cantrybedd level

No. 1 by the crossing gates at Pendre. All trains terminated here when the railway opened, and continued to do so for the quarrymen

J.I.C. Boyd

Left: 'Covered by a close carpet of short mountain turf'. A view of the road bed (*J.I.C. Boyd*). Right: 'Someone had thriftily utilised a discarded saddle tank from TALYLLYN. The platelayers hut (*J.W. Sparrowe*)

means tourists were able to make the 'Grand Tour', as it was called, from Towyn to Machynlleth, the lower terminus of the Corris Railway, and back by the Cambrian Railway.

It is a curious fact that although the Talyllyn Railway was engineered by a member of the celebrated Spooner family and although the terrain was suitable, no attempt ever appears to have been made to adopt the successful Festiniog practice of working loaded slate trains down the line by gravity in charge of brakes-men, and of using locomotives only for the purpose of returning the empties. In spite of a generally favourable gradient, loaded trains were always worked down to Towyn by locomotives. A smaller volume of traffic and the absence of intermediate passing loops may have been the associated reasons for this. Gravity working was certainly not eschewed for any safety reasons, for in connection with tourist traffic a practice far more fraught with possiblities of disaster became common during the holiday season and was perpetuated until quite recent times. This was the arrangement whereby a family party could hire an empty slate wagon for the day. In this they were hauled up the line behind the train and, after the last down train had left Abergynolwyn, they were free to stop and picnic where they would by the lineside before coasting back to Towyn in the evening. This amenity became extremely popular, although its potential dangers scarcely need stressing when we realise that these vehicles were unsprung, that the state of the permanent way left much to be desired, and that for the greater part of its course the line occupies a ledge on the mountain side having an almost sheer drop on one side. It is interesting to speculate upon the reactions of Captain Tyler or his successors in the Railway Inspection department of the Ministry of Transport had they visited Towyn and beheld, either a long train of crowded wagons about to ascend without any adequate means of dealing with the consequences of a derailment or a breakaway, or alternatively the spectacle of a happy family of children and grown-ups bowling merrily homewards down a 1 in 60 gradient in the half light of a summer dusk. They would have been even more concerned had they known that the Company never indulged in such precautions as public liability insurance.

Nor, for that matter, were the locomotive boilers insured. When questioned about such risks: 'We are always very careful,' was the simple answer of the staff. The optimistic few who sought compensation from the Company for minor injuries or shock following wagon derailments were easily dealt with. They were referred to Sir Haydn Jones whose invariable 'No' was so categorical and final that no one ever had the courage to appeal to any higher court. Happily for the management of the Talyllyn Railway, Captain Tyler's cautious blessing of 1866 must have become so deeply embedded in the ministerial filing system that the existence of the little line was forgotten by these admirable guardians of the public safety. Nor, thanks to good luck and beneficent providence, did any disaster occur to draw their attention to the curious operational methods practised in this remote corner of West Wales.

So the years still rolled by uneventfully. Slate traffic dwindled as we have seen. So did local passenger traffic after a regular bus service began to operate between Towyn and Abergynolwyn at fares which were not only lower than the railway's but below those on neighbouring bus routes where there was no steam competitor. But the internal combustion engine which drew local traffic away also brought summer visitors to the district in increasing numbers until tourist traffic became the mainstay of the line. The railway itself was now a part of history and it was no longer the attraction of the Dolgoch ravine or the outworn claim to be the quickest route to anywhere which primarily attracted passengers, but the character of the railway itself. The young it had always fascinated, but for the old it now acquired a nostalgic appeal, reminding them, in a distracted world obsessed with the quantitive and dubious values of speed and size, of the smaller but more stable and assured world which they had known and loved when they were young.

Then for the second time in a generation the twentieth century split into the chaos of a world war and this time the mountains of Merioneth were no barrier against its grim realities. A great military camp sprang up just outside Towyn; aeroplanes throbbed overhead; miles of barbed wire fenced the shores of Cardigan Bay and strange amphibious monsters invaded Corbett's Promenade to rehearse their future landings on the Normandy beaches. This second world war rang down the curtain on many of the minor railways which had managed to survive, as many others had not, the road competition of the 1930s. Even the famous Festiniog line became a casualty. But the Talyllyn Railway carried on in spite of all, and it was during these distracted war years that I first made its acquaintance.

Chapter Two

It was on a fine evening after a day of heavy rain that I came over the pass from Dolgelley and, looking down between the crags which tower above that narrow defile, saw the valley for the first time. There is no finer sight in Wales than this suddenly revealed vision of the lake of Talyllyn sparkling in the setting of its encircling mountains. In the crystalline atmosphere of this evening of sunshine after storm the contrasts of light and shadow on these mountains were almost unbelievably vivid; the majestic face of Craig Goch on the southern shore so golden in sunlight; the slopes of Cader opposite so deep in shadow that night seemed already to have fallen there. After the day's downpour, torrents were everywhere thundering off the mountains in milk-white cascades that glittered like vertical veins of quartz on the dark rocks of cwm or precipice. The reverberations of this falling water filled the evening stillness with a sound like that of a wind in tree tops. Yet in the valley there was sheltered calm. Only on the high skyline of Cader where the streams were leaping into the invisible bowl of Llyn Cae was a wind whipping their spray into the air like plumes of steam.

Weather conditions certainly conspired on this first occasion to show me the valley in its most dramatic mood. Later I was to know it in every seasonal temper: cold and austere in the snows of early spring; tranquil in the blue haze of high summer or melancholy in the mourning veils of rain when trailing cloud curtains covered the mountains almost to lake level. As will appear later, these low flying clouds which all too frequently swept in from the sea to blind the valley in mist and rain were often to be the occasion of difficulty and anxiety on the Talyllyn Railway.

It was not until I had been at Talyllyn a couple of days that it dawned upon me that I was staying only a few miles from the upper terminus of the railway. Moreover, I learnt to my surprise that in spite of the war a passenger service of two trains a day each way was in operation on Mondays, Wednesdays and Fridays. This discovery awakened memories of past journeys on the Festiniog, Welsh Highland, Glyn Valley and Welshpool & Llanfair Railways, and I resolved to renew and enlarge my experience of the narrow gauge forthwith. So I journeyed into Towyn by bus on the Wednesday morning with the object of travelling back as far as Abergynolwyn on the afternoon train and then walking the remainder of the way back to Talyllyn. Unfortunately, however, the walking part of this programme was fated to prove much longer than I anticipated. For when I strolled down to the Wharf station after lunch my hopes were dashed by a small handwritten notice which had been pinned on the board by the station gate. NO TRAIN TO-DAY it stated laconically in characters slightly smudged by haste and rain. So that was that. There was no sign of life. The little red brick office building was locked up and a wet wind from the sea was whipping across the deserted yard. I decided that, rather than wait about in Towyn for the next bus, I would walk back up the valley along the line, so I set off under the Wharf road bridge and through the long waterlogged cutting in the direction of Pendre. Here, where the track fanned out into loop and shed roads, I saw for the first time the ancient four-wheeled coaches. They were at rest in a long narrow open-sided shed which fitted them so nicely and seemed so decrepit that it looked almost as if the coaches were helping to support its undulating slate roof which would collapse behind them if they were withdrawn. Just beyond this was the locomotive shed, and here I discovered signs of life and at the same time an explanation for the absence of any animation elsewhere. An engine was standing in the shed, and beneath her in the gloom of the pit between the rails, my eye caught the flickering light of a tallow candle. The sound of a heavy hammer striking unyielding metal was followed by a spate of rapid Welsh which, to my uninitiated ear, might equally have been instructive, argumentative or merely explosive and profane. Then there was another round of hammering. Thinking back, I believe that the victim of this forceful treatment was No. 1

TALYLLYN, but much as I should have liked to do so, I deemed it tactful not to enter the shed. For I knew only too well from my own experience just how exasperating the appearance of a talkative and inquisitive stranger can be to anyone in desperate travail with obstinate machinery. At any rate the mystery of the missing train was now solved. So I left them to it, walking on past the little station platform and shelter, over the gated level crossing and away up the grass-grown track which, with high hedges on either hand, was more like a country lane than a railway. Just before I came to Rhydyronen station, sheltering in its group of pine trees, I encountered two old men who were carrying out some repairs of a somewhat rudimentary character to the permanent way. They were working with that extreme deliberation which seems to characterise permanent way men wherever there are railways and which makes the work appear to be like some game of chess where each move, if it be only one step forward, must first be carefully pondered. Since it was obvious that whatever might be happening in the motive power department there was certainly no state of emergency here, I stopped to talk to them. But it was at once obvious from their blank expressions that they knew no English.

It did not take me long to reach Brynglas once I had passed under the ivy-covered bridge at Rhydyronen, for the two stations are comparatively close together. But then followed a long two miles to Dolgoch. There was a considerable cutting and an over-bridge beyond Brynglas and then the character of the line changed. For the broader levels near Towyn had been left behind now and instead of a country lane the little railway had become a mountain track, a narrow shelf cut in the lower southern slopes of the valley of the Afon Fathew. Between bushes of thorn and hazel I looked down to the little stream meandering through its marshlands and beyond it to the grey farms and the steeply-tilted patchwork of small fields on the opposite slope of the valley. In places dark bushes of gorse grew so closely beside the wavering line of metals that they threatened to overwhelm them. Beyond the hedge on my right were the steeper bracken covered slopes of the open mountain which swept upward to a bare crown where a buzzard was soaring on motionless wings, borne up like a kite upon ascending air currents. Ahead, the distant peak of Cader Idris played hide-and-seek with its clouds and foothills, now lost, now clear and majestic against the blue. At the approach to Dolgoch there were rock cuttings and oak trees whose branches arched over the track to make a tunnel of green shade. Then suddenly, as though I must needs be reminded that this was no mere mountain trackway but a railway, the line emerged from a cutting and strode proudly across the Dolgoch ravine on its lofty three span viaduct. Below, the stream tore down its rocky channel and to my right, invisible behind a dense screen of trees, I could hear the thunder of the falls. Once across the viaduct another rock cutting, this time on a sharp curve, led me to Dolgoch station where the platform and the little slate-built shelter were almost buried in great bushes of rhododendron which flourished in that peaty soil. Here, too, there stood a leaky wooden tank on a slate column for supplying the engines with water. Now on the last lap of the way, the track took me out of the shelter of the trees and past that quarry siding where disaster had once befallen the quarrymen's train. Having now lost the waters of the Dolgoch stream, the valley below soon became waterless while its slopes were higher and steeper. On my right they rose to a skyline no longer even but jagged with outcropping rocks which had scarred the slopes below with small screes. Here the road bed was completely covered by a close carpet of short mountain turf which left only the line of worn and rusty rails visible, and straying mountain sheep bounded ahead of me along the line. With the exception of the two old platelayers and the wheeling buzzards they were the only life I met on the railway. At one point on this last stretch I passed a small platelayer's shelter; like all the architectural works on the line except the viaduct, some bridge abutments and the Wharf station office, the walls of this shelter were of slate slab, but for a roof someone had thriftily utilised a discarded saddle tank from TALYLLYN.

I had no time on this occasion to explore the mineral extension to Bryn Eglwys. Instead, when I reached the little terminus at Abergynolwyn I struck off down the track to the valley road and the village. So ended my first journey over the Talyllyn Railway. Six years were to pass before I should repeat it as a fare-paying passenger.

The reader will have inferred from my experience that the motive power of the Talyllyn Railway was by this time in a somewhat parlous state. This was indeed the case. The two little Fletcher Jennings locomotives were suffering not only from their excessive burden of years but also from the lack of skilled maintenance. There is little doubt that they were well looked after during the eighteen years of Bousted's reign at Pendre, and after that worthy's departure to Australia a local man named Griffiths was frequently employed on a contract basis to carry out any major repairs or renewals which became necessary. His son, the manager of the local cinema, has shown me his father's old account book in which he kept a detailed record of his activities. This revealed a remarkable versatility, being the case book of a man who was obviously General Practitioner for all things mechanical in Towyn and district. He seems to have been as well acquainted and as competent to deal with the maladies of chapel organs or cottage pianos as with the mysteries of DOLGOCH's patent valve motion. In small towns like Towyn, far removed from industrial areas where the process of specialisation was already far advanced, there was still plenty of scope for versatile master men like Griffiths, and from the records he has left behind him it does not appear that the locomotives suffered any neglect in his hands. With only the most primitive equipment at his disposal no job deterred him. He even cast new bearing brasses on the spot, and some of his wooden patterns for these castings survive to this day as an object lesson in self-sufficiency. But after the departure of Griffiths, and with the progressive decline in the Company's fortunes, it is clear that the locomotives suffered increasingly from the attentions of a succession of unskilled, or at the best semi-skilled and self-taught, drivers. The engines themselves confirmed the evidence of my own ears on my first visit to Pendre: that a heavy hammer had become the most popular tool. Indeed there were very few other tools available. Nevertheless, in fairness to the men concerned, it was remarkable that such self-taught fitters managed to keep these antique locomotives running as long as they did. Part of the credit is due undoubtedly to Messrs Fletcher, Jennings for good workmanship, robust design and quality of materials, but even the best cannot last for ever. Latterly it was a case of 'ignorance is bliss' when the engines continued to work in a condition which, to a locomotive engineer, would have seemed to be tempting providence too far so fraught was it with probabilities of disaster both mechanical and explosive. That no such disaster occurred can only have been due to that unusually beneficent guardian angel who, throughout its long history, seems to have presided over the Company's affairs. But by 1945 matters had reached such a pass that it became obvious at last that neither locomotive could continue to work without a major overhaul. Sir Haydn Jones was not prepared to finance the repair of both engines, and the choice fell upon No. 2, DOLGOCH. She was sent away in April to the Atlas Foundry at Shrewsbury and for twelve months the railway was closed. This was the first serious break in the railway's long record of continuous service, for until then a two days a week service had been continued throughout the winter. But henceforth, though the line was reopened for the summer of 1946, winter running was discontinued. When DOL-GOCH returned, gleaming in fresh green livery, one of her first actions was to become derailed up the line, so that, despite her appalling condition, TALYLLYN had to be steamed and sent out to her rescue. This successful salvage operation was destined to be the last duty performed by TALYLLYN, and those who have subsequently viewed the ominous bulge in the side of her firebox which betokens broken stays, or investigated a smoke-box tube plate which consists of more scale than plate, are of unanimous opinion that he was a brave man who steamed and drove her on this last journey.

Meanwhile during the war years labour had been drifting away from Bryn Eglwys quarry either into the services or into other civil employment. In the new army camp that was growing at Towyn and in the new plantations of Abergynolwyn the Ministry of Works and the Forestry Commission both offered alternative employment that was at once less arduous and hazardous and at the same time better paid than slate quarrying. It was in 1946 that quarrying operations finally ceased at Bryn Eglwys, although for some time after a small quantity of slate continued to travel down to Towyn as existing stocks were cleared. This total eclipse of the slate trade meant that the railway's only hope of survival was the summer tourist traffic.

While these events were taking place other interests were fully absorbing my time and attention. The recollections of my first exploration of the railway, though not forgotten, were relegated to a back page in that album of memories where, like ageing photographs, their definition seemed destined to fade gradually with the passage of time. They became part of a curious collection which included, not only other odd railways and locomotives but steam ploughing engines and archaic pieces of agricultural machinery, racing and veteran motor cars, beam engines, wind and water mills, and boats of assorted shapes and sizes varying from coracles to canal craft. For my interest in things mechanical has always been coupled with the conviction that variety is indeed the spice of life.

The circumstance which led me to turn back to the Talyllyn page in the album sooner than might have been expected was the publication by H.M. Stationery Office of the text of the Transport Bill. I acquired a copy of this primarily to discover what effect it was likely to have on the canal system, but my interest in transport generally led me to wade through the whole text of a measure which, according to the political dogma then prevailing, was going to rescue road, rail and canal transport from the thrall of 'private enterprise' and dedicate them to the especial service of humble British citizens like myself. I studied the list of railway companies which were to be thus liberated with particular interest and found it almost all-embracing. It even included such railway by-ways as the East Kent and the Kent & East Sussex which had been passed over in the railway amalgamation of 1921. But there was one omission, one small by-way which seemed to have been overlooked: the Talyllyn Railway Company was not included. This was surprising in a Bill so comprehensive as to include such ghostly concerns as the Hereford & Gloucester Canal Company whose property is more difficult to trace to-day than Offa's Dyke. The reason may have been partly a financial one, for whereas the shareholders of this lost canal still received a certain sum in compensation from the Great Western Railway, who had built the branch line from Gloucester to Ledbury over a part of their property, the Talyllyn Railway had never become involved in any way with any other transport undertaking. But perhaps also the architects of the Transport Bill were under the impression that the railway was already defunct, for did not the current edition of the Ordnance Survey mark Rhydyronen, Brynglas, Dolgoch and Abergynolwyn stations as closed?

Be that as it may, it was clear that the railway which had seen the dragon and rose entwined of the Cambrian Railway come and go might now live to watch its proud successor, the arms of London and Bristol, the 'Domini dirige Nos' and 'Virtue et Industria' of the Great Western give place to the mean little insignia of British Railways. Moreover, for the first time, the Talyllyn's neighbour would cease officially to be a railway at all and become, in current bureaucratic jargon, 'the Western Region'.

But could this lone survivor of private enterprise manage to live on into this new era? As the old railway companies which I had known and loved were finally dissolved before my eyes I found myself becoming more and more keenly interested in the future of Talyllyn and talked the question over endlessly with two railway-minded friends in Banbury, Bill Trinder and Jim Russell, both of whom had in the past served the late lamented Great Western Railway Company. Neither had seen the Talyllyn and both became anxious to do so. So there began a series of visits to Towyn in the course of which we made the acquaintance of Sir Haydn Jones, his second in command Mr Edward Thomas and various other interested local people. The first of these visits was made in the early part of the year when the line was not working, so once again I walked its length, this time including the extension from Abergynolwyn to the foot of Alltwyllt incline. But on the next occasion it was summer and for the first time I was able to make the journey as a fare-paying passenger.

I shall not forget my first and only meeting with Sir Henry Haydn Jones which took place in his large office over the post office at Towyn where, like some old eagle in his eyrie, he could look out over the centre of the town. Ushered into this retreat by way of the ironmonger's shop which he owned, I found him sitting before one of two large desks both of which were stuffed and piled with papers. It was as though, having more than exhausted the capacity of one desk, the simplest solution had been to move on to another. With a fine head of snow-white hair, and wearing a fly-away collar, black coat and striped trousers which I felt sure had seen service in the House of Commons, Sir Haydn immediately impressed me as being a large figure in more than the mere physical sense of that word, although in physical stature alone he was striking enough. I have learned since that one of his characteristics was a remarkable ability to concentrate upon several different matters at once, a mental gift which I, for one, conspicuously lack. Callers were apt to be disconcerted and over-awed when he engaged them in conversation while he continued to write with undiminished speed. Happily he did not treat me to a demonstration of this curious gift or I am sure it would have had such an effect upon me. But though I was spared such a display of mental gymnastics, his conversation left me in no doubt that his eighty years had not in any way blunted the sharpness of his wits. He spoke without sentiment and to the point. He was losing money on the railway, but so long as he lived he would continue to run a summer service. He would welcome any suggestion which might help to ensure the future life of the line but he did not see that anything could be done short of the expenditure of a large sum of money with little prospect of any commensurate return.

I subsequently heard Sir Haydn referred to locally as a man who was respected but not loved. Upon the justice of this summing up one brief interview does not qualify me to comment. But I was left with the impression that Sir Haydn was as typical of the Victorian age as the railway which he had so long controlled. And so completely has our social philosophy changed since then that perhaps we tend only to see the faults of the Victorians and to

Left: 'characteristic representative of the long and illustrious seafaring tradition'. John Parry in conversation with Clough Williams Ellis a decade later (*Robin Butterell*). Right: 'Secretary, Accountant, Booking Clerk Station Master and Guard'. Mr Edward Thomas at the time of the author's early visits (*Daily Express*)

'Mr Edward Thomas was a small man quick and bird-like in his movements'. Edward Thomas aged seventeen outside the Wharf office with his father Hugh and guard Jacob Rowlands

'Admitted he had merely driven up to see if the rails were still there'. The old winding house on the mineral extension above Abergynolwyn

T.R. Archive, photo J.F. Rimmer

'Now in its desolation it had become not merely a lonely but an eerie place, haunted by evidence of past activity.' The author's duck's back Alvis in Bryn Eglwys quarry

J.B. Snell

ignore their virtues. A future generation may see them in a clearer and more just perspective.

Ever since he had acquired control in 1911, Sir Haydn had delegated the responsibility of running the railway entirely to Mr Edward Thomas, a man whose association with the Company extended back to 1897. Physically and in character the two men were quite unlike each other, for Mr Thomas was a small man, quick and bird-like in his movements and not in the least awe-inspiring. But the years had dealt as lightly with him as with his master, and a few moments conversation with him left no doubt that Sir Haydn had placed the practical management of the line in extremely capable hands. He had keen but very kindly blue eyes and great natural courtesy of manner which was quite unforced and unselfconscious. He spoke always to the point in a voice as quick and precise as his every movement, frequently punctuating statements of fact with the characteristic Welsh interrogative 'Isn't it?' which sometimes sounds to English ears irrelevant and ungrammatical, but which the Welshman uses to drive a point home as we should say 'Is that not so?' But there is no occasion thus to speak of Mr Edward Thomas in the past tense since he is happily still very much with us. On many occasions in the time to come I should have cause to be grateful for the unfailing help and kindness shown to me by this remarkably astute mind and shrewd judge of character.

With the skeleton staff to which the Talyllyn Railway had been reduced, Mr Thomas's job during the summer running season was no easy sinecure. He was Secretary, Accountant, Booking Clerk, Station Master and Guard all rolled into one. When I first saw him, clad in the neat grey tweed suit he always affects, he was busy selling tickets for the afternoon train at Towyn Wharf station. When the last passenger had been booked in he clapped on his trilby hat, locked up the office and walked briskly towards the waiting train with the cash takings in a linen bag tightly clasped by the neck. Before hopping nimbly into the brake-van it was his invariable custom to signal the 'right away' by a quick, per-emptory flick of the wrist of his free hand, as though he were shoo-ing the train away like some disobedient dog. This little gesture seemed to be just as effective as the more orthodox ritual of whistle and flag, for it was immediately answered by a shrill toot from DOLGOCH. Then with a sigh of steam from cylinder cocks and leaking glands and the creak and snatch of tautening couplings, the ancient train gathered itself together and lumbered away under the bridge on yet another journey up the valley.

In spite of the shocking deterioration of the permanent way, the overall schedule of 45 minutes from start to final stop which had prevailed for many years was still maintained. A ridiculously easy timing by any ordinary railway standards, it was quite otherwise on such a road as this. The old four-wheelers reeled along, pitching, rolling and bumping over the rough rail joints. It seemed, too, that wherever there was a particularly steep and deep declivity on the valley side of the line the rails canted alarmingly in that direction so that the coaches felt as though they were teetering top-heavily on the very brink.

On arrival at Abergynolwyn it was the custom for the locomotive to detach itself from the train and to run on up the mineral extension as far as the site of the original locomotive shed. Here the waters of a mountain stream had been diverted by an open wooden trough to the top of a stone pillar at the line side whence, by means of another portable length of troughing, it could be fed into the engine tank. After one of our trips up the line from Towyn in the early summer of 1949, Bill Trinder and I decided when we reached Abergynolwyn station that we would walk on up the line behind the locomotive. We had had a particularly stirring journey in every sense of the word, for on this occasion our driver was a local youth of not more than eighteen years who, with an apparently boundless faith in the railway's guardian angel, had succeeded in improving substantially on the scheduled running time. When we reached the water column, if such it could be called, we discovered to our surprise that DOLGOCH had disappeared. Two dark, bruised lines in the long grass which completely covered the disused metals in the direction of Bryn Eglwys showed plainly where the engine had gone; so we walked on, being curious to discover the purpose of this journey. We eventually came upon DOLGOCH standing at the foot of the first incline up to the quarries, at the limit, that is to say, of locomotive working. In answer to our obvious question her driver cheerfully admitted that he had merely driven up to see whether the rails were still there. In view of the fact that some of these rails occupy a narrow ledge from which there is an almost sheer drop of nearly 150 feet into the ravine of the Nant Gwernol, it struck us both very forcibly that there were safer ways of finding this out. However, since the engine had come up safely it should be able to return, so we accepted the driver's invitation to go back with him and joined him and his even more youthful fireman on the footplate. As the engine lurched along the narrow and scarcely visible track, pounding over the uneven rail joints with a series of crashes which made the whole cab rattle, it was disconcerting to look down from the footplate to the churning waters of the Nant Gwernol so far below and to see, wedged between boulders in the stream bed, the mangled remains of smashed wagons, the victims of past breakaways on the incline. At one particularly alarming moment Bill was moved to grab the handbrake only to be informed politely that he might turn it as much as he wished because this, the only orthodox means of arresting DOLGOCH's progress, did not work. That this young driver shortly afterwards left the service of the Company under a cloud is not to be wondered at.

Only a few weeks later I visited the valley again, this time to show the railway to David Curwen, an interested locomotive engineer friend of mine. On a glorious summer morning we arrived in my car at Abergynolwyn with the idea of travelling down to Towyn by the down morning train and returning after lunch. But though we waited for half an hour or more on the little platform there was neither sight nor sound of any train. Eventually we drove on down to the sheds at Towyn Pendre to find out what had happened. After my recent experience I was not unduly surprised to learn that our youthful driver had finished his brief and headlong career by breaking DOLGOCH's frame. As a result, train services had to be suspended during the height of the holiday season until the frame had been repaired, a calamity which seriously affected the 1949 traffic receipts.

Because we could not travel on the railway, David and I were left with time in hand and so we were able for the first time to explore thoroughly the old quarry at Bryn Eglwys. It was destined to be the first of several visits which we made together, for the place held a strange fascination for us. Even in its busy heyday the quarry must have been a wild and lonely place, so remote was it from the world below in its high cleft in the mountains. But now in its desolation it had become not merely a lonely but an eerie place, haunted by the evidence of past activity. For when the last quarryman went his way, all had been left exactly as it stood. The doors of the cottages where a few of the men had lived stood invitingly ajar and the glass in their windows was intact. In the millwrights' shop beside cold hearth and silent anvil the blacksmith's setts lay ready to his hand, while the bed and the lead screws of a lathe still gleamed with oil, the traverses moving easily. A tally book lay open on the desk in the checker's office, and in a winding house a home-made chair awaited the return of the occupant who had painstakingly carved his initials in the stonework of the wall above it. In the 'barracks' where once the men had fed and slept latchless doors slammed in the wind or in lighter airs creaked mournfully on their hinges. A dartboard hung on the wall of the messroom and there was a large black kettle on the crane over the hearth. Outside the buildings the two great water wheels which had driven the air compressors stood forlornly motionless and dry, the water supply cut off from the rotting troughs of their headraces, while trucks, some loaded with slate slab, rested on rusty tracks as if halted in mid-journey. All these things seemed to people Bryn Eglwys with ghosts. It was as though its busy occupants had on a sudden been spirited away into the mountains, while the solitude and the stillness of the old quarry bred the disquieting fancy that they might suddenly, like troglodytes, appear from dark, dripping tunnels, from vertiginous shafts or from the chasms of open workings and collapsed subterranean chambers. But only the occasional melancholy piping of a curlew, the chink and murmur of falling water or the booming of the mountain wind about the gable ends could ever be heard in the long cutting sheds where stood the rows of motionless slate saws and guillotines.

Could the quarry ever be reopened? The question so intimately affected the future of the railway that I sent an enquiry to Mr Cosmo Clark, Director of the Rural Industries Bureau, who most kindly instructed his North Wales representative to make an inspection and report. This document made it only too clear to me that the Talyllyn Railway could never again hope for any traffic from Bryn Eglwys. Since then Welsh wind and weather and the activities of the scrap merchant have between them played havoc with the old quarry and its buildings are now so bare and ruinous that they have lost much of their mystery.

Behind all these explorations, inquiries and meetings lay the question of whether anything could be done to enable the railway to survive. The one great difficulty appeared to me to be the bad state of the permanent way. It really needed completely relaying throughout, and the current prices of steel and timber were such that the cost of this in materials alone would be quite prohibitive. The problem seemed insuperable, and in trying to think of some way round it I conceived the idea of following the example of the Eskdale Railway in Cumberland which had converted its narrow gauge track to the miniature gauge of fifteen inches. Between Towyn Pendre and Abergynolwyn the line would be relaid with miniature track to a gauge of $10\frac{1}{4}$ inches, while between Pendre and the Wharf the line would be 'gauntleted', that is to say both gauges would be retained, one inside the other. By virtue of their great historical interest the old locomotives and stock of the Talyllyn would thus be retained and could be run over this short section. From the purely practical and financial point of view this scheme had much to commend it. Using light miniature rail the cost of relaying both in materials and labour would be vastly reduced and would also be offset by the sale of almost all the old line for scrap. Moreover, despite their diminutive size it was calculated that a 'free-lance' $10\frac{1}{4}$ inch gauge locomotive of modern six-coupled design, hauling roller bearing bogie stock, could handle the same pay load as the old train and operate a faster schedule with much greater economy. But it was obvious that whatever practical engineering and financial advantages such a scheme might possess it would wholly destroy the character of the

Talyllyn Railway as the sole survivor of a railway era which was otherwise extinct. Admittedly the old locomotives and rolling-stock would survive, but they would survive only as museum pieces and for the rest the line would differ only in length from the 'toy railways' which can be found in the pleasure parks of many seaside resorts. It therefore seemed unlikely that such a proposal would win the sympathy of the public on whose support the success of any scheme must depend. Moreover we estimated that to relay the whole line, even using this light second-hand material, would cost £10,000 at current prices. The only alternative, and it seemed a very risky one, would be to launch an appeal for the maintenance of the railway in its present form and to hope that the response would be sufficient to enable some progressive policy of improvement to be undertaken.

At this point in our deliberations I decided to sound public opinion by writing a tentative letter to the press, and as a result of this I received a surprising number of replies expressing interest and promising support. These I filed for future reference. Sir Haydn had given us an undertaking that the railway would not close down so long as he lived, so for the moment it did not seem that anything further could be done. This was in the autumn of 1949, but in the following summer the whole situation was changed overnight by the news of the death of Sir Haydn. As soon as possible after we heard these sad tidings, Bill and I paid a hurried visit to Towyn and interviewed Mr Edward Thomas. We found the railway operating its usual three days per week summer service and carrying a record number of passengers. But Mr Thomas expressed the opinion that while this service would be continued until the end of September, it was extremely unlikely that Sir Haydn's Executors would consider reopening the railway again the following year. On the contrary it was more than probable that the line would be sold up as scrap metal. It was thus obvious that the anticipated but long deferred crisis was now at hand in the shape of a most ignominious end, and that if there were to be any further chapters in the long history of the Talyllyn Railway Company it was now up to us to think and act quickly.

Accordingly, soon after our return from this visit, I wrote to the local solicitor who was acting for the Executors in the matter of Sir

'Could the quarry ever be reopened?' The author with the last two quarrymen, David Roberts and John Evans

Rolt Archive

'. . . trucks, some loaded with slate slab, rested on rusty tracks as if halted in mid-journey.' Houses on the Cantrybedd level of the quarry

W.G. Trinder

'Sir Haydn was as typical of the Victorian age as the railway which he had so long controlled.' Sir Henry Haydn Jones MP in his office at Towyn

'But at long last things were now moving from the sphere of talk to practical action'. DOLGOCH at Wharf station. From left to right: David Curwen (driver), Bill Trinder, P.B. Whitehouse, Tom Rolt and Patrick Garland

Haydn's estate and requested him to obtain the views of the Executors on the following proposals which I outlined. That a voluntary society should be formed to operate the railway on a non-profit making basis, assisting the Company in two ways, by direct subsidy from moneys raised by subscription and by the voluntary work of its members. Whether the Society would acquire the Company outright from the Executors or operate it upon some joint basis with them would depend upon subsequent discussion. The reply to this suggestion was favourable and encouraging.

So far it had been a case of three interested individual enthusiasts pursuing inquiries in a purely tentative and informal manner. But it was now obvious that, with no financial resources of our own, we could not take the next step of arranging a formal discussion with the Executors unless our ideas had the blessing and the backing of a properly constituted committee. I therefore drafted a circular calling for a public meeting at the Imperial Hotel, Birmingham, a copy of which was sent to all those who had already written to me about the railway and to all the railway minded acquaintances we could muster.

This meeting was a great success and the large room we had hired for the purpose was full. Bill Trinder acted as Chairman and was supported on the platform by Mr Edward Thomas, Jim Russell and myself. Mr Thomas, particularly, impressed us all by the way he spoke and by his obviously sincere concern that our efforts would prove successful and enable the railway to continue. There was no lack of contributions from the body of the meeting and these varied from constructive proposals on questions of detail to more sweeping and less practical suggestions. Notable among the latter was an idea that the railway might in future be electrically operated from a hydro-electric generating station harnessing the power of the Dolgoch waterfalls.

I recall with particular amusement the behaviour of one member of the audience. Not only did this gentleman ask a number of pertinent but abstruse financial questions which we were quite unable to answer, but throughout the proceedings he trained upon the unfortunate occupants of the platform an unwavering and baleful stare which seemed to radiate intense suspicion. As he was seated in the front row it was almost impossible to ignore this scrutiny which became almost hypnotic in its effect. I began to feel as if I was acting the part of an unscrupulous company promoter, and it was clear that the others felt the same, for Jim suddenly got to his feet and made his one contribution to the meeting which was to announce in forceful tones that we had not come to Birmingham to sell anyone a gold brick. When the gentleman responsible for provoking this statement later became a member of the Committee we discovered that this expression of acute suspicion was habitual to him and was directed at the world in general and not at us in particular. There was a sequel to this episode on the following Christmas morning when Jim found on his doorstep a gilded brick, suitably wrapped and inscribed by an anonymous donor.

The meeting concluded with the appointment of an investigating committee empowered to open negotiations with Sir Haydn's Executors, and with this appointment the Talyllyn Railway Preservation Society can be said to have been launched. One member of this newly elected Committee suggested that we should start an appeal fund immediately by making a collection at the meeting, but we thought it wiser to turn down this suggestion. For the position was a difficult one. While a knowledge that we had some tangible measure of public financial support behind us would have helped us in our negotiations, it appeared to me to be essential that we should reach some firm basis of agreement with the Executors before any public appeal was launched. We would look supremely foolish if we succeeded in raising a considerable sum of money by public subscription only to find afterwards that our scheme was unworkable. So, although time was perilously short if the railway was to reopen for the 1951 season, it was deemed more prudent to hold our hands for the time being. But we had such high hopes of success that while negotiations were still going on I drafted a combined appeal leaflet and membership form and proposed that members of the Society should enjoy free travel on the railway on production of their membership cards as some return for their support.

The ensuing winter and early spring saw much coming and going between Banbury, Birmingham and Towyn. It became apparent that Lady Haydn Jones, like Mr Edward Thomas, was as anxious as we were to see the railway continue and for this reason she was most generously prepared freely to allow the Society to operate the railway for a trial period of three years, after which time the measure of our success would determine the long term future. Such generosity was an immense help, for it meant that such funds as we might succeed in raising could be entirely devoted to maintenance and improvement. But from the legal and constitutional point of view the situation was not so straight-forward as it had appeared when I had made my first tentative proposal to Lady Haydn's solicitor. For, like its larger brothers which had now been swallowed up by the Transport Act, the Talyllyn Railway was a Statutory Company established by a special Act of Parliament, and it appeared that no radical change in its constitution could be made without promoting a Private Bill. This would be very costly, and in any case we did not wish to change or destroy the identity of so old a company. This problem, for which there was no past precedent, was solved by an arrange-ment whereby a Limited Company, to be called Talyllyn Holdings, Ltd., would be formed for no other purpose than to hold the shares in the old Company which had previously been held by Sir Haydn Jones. Both the Railway Company and the Holdings Company would be administered by a joint directorship consisting of two representatives of the Executors and three from the Society, one of the latter to act as Chairman.

This scheme was thrashed out in the course of a long discussion which took place in Banbury between Jim Russell, myself and Patrick Garland who was to become the extremely capable Treasurer of the Society and of the Company. It was approved shortly afterwards, in early February, 1951, at a joint meeting held in the office of Lady Haydn's solicitor at Machynlleth. Lady Haydn herself and Mr Edward Thomas were to represent the Executors while the Committee appointed its three Directors with Bill Trinder as the Chairman. The successful outcome of this meeting was the signal to launch our appeal for funds. Letters went out to *The Times* and other appropriate sections of the press, national or technical, while our leaflets were circulated to the members of railway and engineering societies all over the country. Money began to come in, not only from every corner of Great Britain but from exiled Welshmen and railway enthusiasts overseas who had known and loved the railway in the past.

If this brief account of the wordy prelude to our railway adventure has wearied the reader he will the more readily be able to sympathise with the sense of frustration which I felt at times during this period when it seemed that the original highly practical object in view would never be achieved and that the railway would rust away in its lonely valley, while the energy which might have re-animated it was unfruitfully dissipated in everlasting letter writing and endless talk in committee rooms thick with tobacco smoke and far removed from the clear mountain air of West Wales. But at long last things were now moving from the sphere of talk to practical action in the actual business of running a railway. If the railway was to be in a fit state to reopen for traffic in the coming summer, things would certainly have to move very rapidly indeed.

Chapter Three

Our newly formed Society was confronted by two major problems which called for immediate solution. First and foremost loomed the fact that we must obtain from somewhere a supply of rails and sleepers in order to start the vitally necessary work of permanent way improvement. Secondly there was the problem of obtaining additional motive power. The condition of engine No. 1 TALYLLYN was so bad that any idea of restoring her to good running order had to be dismissed as financially out of the question. On the other hand it seemed altogether too optimistic to expect one eighty-six years old locomotive to maintain unaided the more ambitious summer train service which we had in mind. DOLGOCH had only run the previous thrice weekly service with difficulty, and the 1949 disaster when she had been crippled at the height of the season was still fresh in memory. In the search for a solution to both these problems our attention very naturally turned to the neighbouring Corris Railway. It was extremely fortunate for us that the Talyllyn possessed so near a neighbour of the same rare gauge of 2 ft. 3 ins. The only other example of a public railway of such a gauge in Great Britain was the Campbelltown & Machrihanish in the faraway Mull of Kintyre and that was long defunct. This meant that the acquisition of locomotives or rolling-stock from any source other than the Corris line would almost certainly involve the added difficulty and expense of gauge conversion. This was the long deferred consequence of the Talyllyn Company's failure to adopt the common 1 ft. $11\frac{1}{2}$ ins. gauge of the Festiniog Railway.

As a horse tramway the history of the Corris goes back further than that of the Talyllyn Railway, but the latter had been running for some years before the Corris adopted steam traction. Having done so, however, the Corris pursued a more energetic passenger traffic policy than its neighbour. Not only did they operate more trains, but the service of horse-drawn wagonettes which was introduced between Corris and Talyllyn Lake was superseded at an early date by motor omnibuses which formed the nucleus of quite an extensive system of road motor services operated by the Corris Company. Thus while the more conservative and retiring Talyllyn never attracted anyone with an eye to business in the transport world, the more ambitious Corris was bought up by the Bristol Tramways when the latter were expanding their road interests in competition with the G.W.R. Eventually, however, the Bristol company surrendered the Corris to the Great Western as part of a 'knock-for-knock' agreement. So it came about that, as an insignificant offshoot of the Great Western, the Corris Railway was nationalised under the terms of the Transport Act. The period following the passing of this measure has been marked, not only by a tremendous increase in transport charges but by a more ruthless pruning of unremunerative branch lines than ever private enterprise had undertaken. The Corris, however, had already felt the axe. Traffic had been suspended in 1947, the reason given being that the abnormal flooding of the Dovey following the heavy snows of that winter had undermined the approach embankment to the bridge by which the railway crossed that river near Machynlleth. By the time our Society came into being the Corris rails had, unfortunately, already been sold to a local scrap merchant, while of the bridge over the Dovey only the stone piers remained. Before the bridge was dismantled, the two surviving locomotives had been moved from their shed at Maespoeth, where they would otherwise have been cut off, to Machynlleth yard. Together with the goods brake-van and the few open goods wagons which constituted all the surviving rolling-stock (for passenger services on the Corris had ceased many years before) they remained the property of the Railway Executive.

We decided to purchase from the scrap merchant as much Corris rail as we could afford, although at the price demanded this could only be a tithe of the quantity needed. A number of Corris sleepers were also bought, and by late spring this material had been laid on a section of the Talyllyn between Fach Goch and Cynfal Halts which thereafter was always referred to as 'the Corris Straight'. The question which remained to be considered was whether the two Corris engines would solve our motive power problem and if so whether we could afford to buy one or both of them. They were reputed to be in a bad state of repair, while the price asked was said to be £65 each. The outlook was therefore not too promising, but it was agreed that Jim Russell, myself and David Curwen, who had been appointed our Chief Mechanical Engineer, should go to Machynlleth and inspect them.

Both were 0–4–2 saddle tank engines. The older was the sole survivor of the three original Corris locomotives which had been supplied to the railway by Hughes of Loughborough in 1878. This firm later passed through two changes of ownership in the course of which it became known as the Falcon Engineering and Car Works. Consequently, although the locomotive was known officially simply as 'No. 3', she was often referred to colloquially as 'The Falcon'. The second engine, No. 4, was a much more recent acquisition, having been built by Messrs Kerr, Stuart and Co., of Stoke-on-Trent in 1921. By this firm she was called a 'Tattoo Special', being a slightly modified version of a standard type known by the code name of 'Tattoo'.

As the three of us motored westwards over the by now well known road across the border hills on a cold bright morning in earliest spring, I found myself pondering on the strange turns and patterns of life whereby people or things which have been lost in the past reappear many years later to play a far more important and unforeseeable role. For almost exactly twenty-two years before, when I was serving my apprenticeship with Kerr Stuart & Co., my mate in the boiler shop where I was then working had been sent down to Machynlleth to carry out some boiler repairs to one of the two engines I was now going to see. I recalled how I had hoped against hope that I might be allowed to accompany him, and my acute disappointment when the hierarchy of chargehand, shop foreman and manager had decreed otherwise. I do not think my mate had ever ventured so far afield from his native Stoke-on-Trent before, and because his broad Staffordshire tongue persisted in calling his destination 'Makinilek', he experienced some difficulty in reaching a place which, so far as he was concerned, might have been in the antipodes. On his return, when he related his adventures to me in graphic detail and expressed decided views upon the mysteries of the Welsh tongue, I remembered how much I had envied him an experience I had been unable to share. Little did I think then that my acquaintance with this particular locomotive was eventually destined to be far more intimate and prolonged than his, although by that time the firm of Kerr Stuart would have long ago ceased to exist.

Our first glimpse of the two engines in the searching sunlight of that March morning was not encouraging. They stood head to tail on the short length of track in Machynlleth yard which was all that now remained of the Corris Railway. They had been covered with old wagon sheets, but, as rust and broken spectacle and gauge glass showed, these had not adequately protected them either from the weather or from those inevitable hooligans who can never see a piece of glass without smashing it. But these first impressions were superficial and a closer examination revealed that the engines were not in such bad condition as we had been led to suppose. Of the two, the older engine appeared to be in the better order, but on both the motion looked in reasonable condition and someone had had the forethought to protect rods and slide bars with grease. Although she was actually the heavier and had larger diameter driving wheels, No. 3 appeared the smaller engine and possessed a ridiculously undersized pair of trailing wheels, like castors, under a cab which looked as if it had been made for dwarfs. As was the case with TALYLLYN, these trailing wheels were a subsequent addition, but why the overall height of the locomotive was so severely limited is a mystery, as the loading gauge on the Corris was not unduly restricted.

With all old locomotives it is the condition of the boiler which is the critical factor that usually decides their fate. Given a fair standard of maintenance, what might be called the 'chassis' of a locomotive is so robust by comparison with other more modern machines such as the motor car that its life can be prolonged almost indefinitely. But it is quite otherwise with the boiler which not only has a limited life, but is peculiarly prone to suffer in many ways from neglect and maltreatment or from feed water of bad quality. Moreover the cost of reboilering nowadays is prohibitive. Unfortunately it is impossible accurately to assess the condition of a boiler without stripping it completely of its lagging which, in engines of this type, means removing the saddle tank, the bunkers and most of the cab. Yet so far as we could see from peering through smoke box and firebox doors the Falcon's boiler seemed to be in fair order although she might need a new set of tubes.

In the case of No. 4 it was quite otherwise. Although a much younger engine it was apparent that she had been worked much harder, worked almost to death in fact. Where her plates and seams were visible they showed ominous signs of wastage, complete retubing was obviously essential, while an inspection door had been removed to reveal that all was not well with her firebox crown stays. Yet David expressed the opinion that the boiler was repairable so far as he could judge. Assuming that this was so, No. 4 looked the better proposition of the two for our purpose. Because she was one of a standard type which Kerr Stuarts had built in quantity for contractors' use, she had been designed on extremely simple lines with a view to ease of maintenance and replacement. For example, unlike No. 3, whose inside Stephenson's link valve motion was concealed neatly but inaccessibly between the frames, No. 4's valve gear was outside and was of an extremely simple type which was called by the makers 'modified Hackworth'. The result might not be aesthetically pleasing, indeed the shameless exposure of all its vital organs combined with the absence of a continuous line of footplating from cab to front buffer beam gave the engine a trans-Atlantic appearance, but such simplicity and accessibility would be valuable qualities in view of the primitive repair equipment available at Towyn. She was also fitted with sanding gear controlled from the cab, a refinement lacking on No. 3 and on the Talyllyn locomotives. In another important respect both Corris engines surpassed their more primitive neighbours on the Talyllyn, for they were fitted with power brakes. No. 3 had vacuum brakes while No. 4 had the standard type of steam brake interconnected to vacuum gear which had been specially fitted to the engine to supply the train pipe on the Corris passenger rolling-stock which had vanished long ago. One point which we failed to notice about the 'Falcon' was that the treads of her wheel tyres were half an inch narrower than those on No. 4 or on the Talyllyn engines. We may perhaps be forgiven for not observing a detail which sounds so trivial as I set it down here, yet this seemingly insignificant difference of dimension was destined to be the cause of an unbelievable amount of trouble, anxiety, disappointment and sheer hard labour in the months to come.

Sixty-five pounds may not sound a lot of money for a locomotive, as indeed it is not, but it was felt that owing to unavoidable expenditure on permanent way we could not afford to buy both at this figure when the cost of rail carriage to Towyn had to be considered also. So when we duly reported on our visit, the Committee were faced with a decision as difficult as the judgment of Paris. On the one hand there was a locomotive in reasonable order which could be put into steam fairly quickly and at moderate expense; on the other there was a machine requiring an expensive overhaul that would take time, but which ultimately promised to be by far the better of the two for our purpose. So insoluble was this problem that Bill, Jim and I finally volunteered to go to Swindon and plead our case in the hope that we might thereby get the price down to a figure which would enable us to buy both engines.

Bill lost no time in arranging an appointment with the Chief Stores Superintendent at Swindon, and as we journeyed south from Banbury through the little grey towns of Burford and Lechlade to the great railway citadel of brick and steel which Gooch, Dean and Churchward have made famous we reflected upon the many unsuspected channels into which our interest in one small and remote Welsh railway was leading us. On arrival we were conducted by a bewildering route through echoing subways, up and down steps and along lineside paths beside a maze of tracks to a typical railway office which, with its massive mahogany furniture, still radiated the dignified but assured air of commercial prosperity of the Victorian age when the railway monopoly of land transport seemed unassailable. Here Bill stated our case with such eloquence and feeling that I really believe that if Swindon had still been the domain of the Great Western Railway we might have had both engines given to us. But alas, we could no longer appeal to a Chief Mechanical Engineer presiding with undisputed sway over the affairs of Swindon. For in this strange age of ours individual greatness is a quality unpopular and 'undemocratic', and it is no longer considered seemly for one man to wield so much authority. So the succession of famous men who had done so much to make the Western Railway Great was ended and the responsibilities of their office divided between three officials who were in turn responsible, to a degree that no C.M.E. ever was to his directors, to a hierarchy of committees. These harassed and sorely tried men, however well disposed they might feel towards us, were not empowered to give us anything, and if we were seeking a donation they could only refer us elsewhere with the warning that months might elapse before any decision was reached. But that they were sympathetic towards us was obvious, and after conferring together privately while we waited in acute suspense, we were told that they had decided that they could write them off their books at a figure much lower than that originally named. It was a figure which would enable us to acquire both engines for less than the previous price of one. This most generous gesture was better than anything we had seriously hoped for when we set out on this mission and we were in high spirits as we drove back, feeling that the afternoon's work had set us well on the way to a solution of the motive power problem.

As soon as the result of our visit to Swindon was known, the Committee decided to purchase both Corris engines, their cost being covered by generous donations made by individual members. At the same time an enthusiast in Leeds who had already purchased the Corris brake-van with the intention of preserving it but had not taken delivery, very handsomely donated it to the Talyllyn Railway in lieu of a financial subscription to the Society. It was therefore decided to purchase the Corris goods wagons also, as they would make a very valuable addition to the motley collection of old slate wagons on the Talyllyn. Arrangements were made for the locomotives and all these vehicles to be shipped by rail from Machynlleth to Towyn Wharf.

In spite of the state of the permanent way, the uncertain locomotive position and the fact that none of us had had practical experience of running any railway larger than a miniature or a model, we were determined to reopen the Talyllyn Railway as usual for the summer season and to maintain this time a five days a week service, leaving only Saturdays and Sundays clear for maintenance work. To reopen was essential not only to maintain continuity of working but to earn some revenue to swell our slender resources. Whether the railway would successfully stand the strain of another whole season of more frequent running without more attention than we had either the time or the money to give it was a very large question, but it was a gamble which we had to take.

It was at this time, in the early spring, that the Committee asked me whether I would go down to Towyn for the season to act as general manager in succession to Mr Edward Thomas. The prospect filled me with considerable trepidation when I thought of Mr Thomas's long experience, my own inexperience and the hundred and one things which could go wrong. However, it appeared that I was the only person who could take the job on, being the only member of the Committee who was, to use official jargon, a 'self-employed person'. Never in the course of my lifelong interest in railways had I ever dreamed that I would one day be called upon to take charge of a real public railway within the meaning of the Act. It promised to be a unique experience, and does not such varied experience constitute the real riches of life? So I argued and so I accepted the post. What, I wondered, did the next few months hold in store for us? Would our efforts succeed in adding yet another worthy chapter to the railway's long record of continuous service, or would they end ignominiously in some catastrophic derailment or irremediable locomotive failure? Not if I could help it. The railway should run the season through if it was humanly possible, but I piously hoped that the railway's over-worked guardian angel had not retired like Mr Thomas from active duty but would join my staff.

Before I was able to establish myself at Towyn for the season it was the month of May and in the meantime very considerable

'We waited in acute suspense and were told they could write them off their books at a figure much lower than that originally named.' The two purchased Corris engines after their arrival at Wharf station

J.I.C. Boyd

'A valuable addition to the permanent staff'. John Snell in conversation with Bill Oliver at Pendre

Daily Express

'Assisted by willing bands of volunteers'. Lifting rails on the disused furnicular down to the village of Abergynolwyn

Left: 'With such a face . . . he should have been a Bard or Arch Druid'. Peter Williams at Pendre crossing gates

progress had been made. The two existing employees of the railway, Hugh Jones and his son Dai, reinforced by additional labour from the neighbouring miniature railway at Fairbourne, had put in a considerable amount of work on the permanent way between Towyn and Rhydyronen. At the same time, Bill Oliver, a member of the committee who lived locally, had been lifting rails on the disused funicular down to the village of Abergynolwyn assisted at week-ends by willing bands of volunteers. Having never been used by locomotives, these rails were comparatively unworn and would make a valuable addition to our stock of permanent way material. Meanwhile Pendre locomotive shed proudly displayed an unprecedented array of locomotive power which was certainly impressive even though it was as yet only potential. For the two Corris engines had arrived and had been hauled thither by DOLGOCH from the Wharf where they had been unloaded by crane. David Curwen was already at work at Pendre, fitting a mechanical lubricator to DOLGOCH and stripping her boiler for inspection before turning his attention to the Corris engines. Assisting David was John Snell, an enthusiast who had just finished his last term at Bryanston School and who had written to me some time previously to ask whether he could work on the railway until he went up to Oxford in the autumn. Though fresh from school and therefore quite unskilled, in looks, in manners and in sheer height and size John appeared to be much older than his age. Perhaps it was because of his size that he seemed lethargic both in speech and action. I could imagine no catastrophe of fire, flood or sudden death dire enough to make John show any excitement or quicken his normal pace. Yet although his manner scarcely betrayed the fact, he was one of the keenest of enthusiasts, and during the months to come he was to prove a most valuable addition to what might be called 'the permanent staff'.

Our activities on the railway had naturally aroused local curiosity, and with the object of satisfying this and at the same time rousing local support a public meeting had been held in Towyn at Easter. This had been very successful and had produced quite a crop of subscriptions, some for life membership. There were fervent speeches in Welsh as well as English and the proceedings had terminated in the singing of both National Anthems. Even those local people who made no financial contribution seemed one and all to be well disposed and sympathetic towards us, and I soon found that I could not enter a shop or a Bank in the little town without being greeted by the solicitous inquiry: 'How's the little railway?' as though I was a nurse or a doctor coaxing back to life a difficult case. Two of our local sympathisers, John Parry and Peter Williams, I would mention especially here for they were to prove themselves supporters of the railway as staunch and as helpful in their different ways as Mr Edward Thomas.

John Parry was Mr Thomas's nephew although he was considerably older than this relationship might lead one to suppose. Like his uncle he was unmarried and the two shared a house close to the Wharf station. He had spent many years at sea, and even if his clear eyes, which often twinkled with amusement, or the swinging gait of his short, stocky figure failed to betray this association, a visit to his home could leave no shadow of doubt about it. For there was a mast and halyards on the law, a binnacle in the front porch, and outside the back door a lifebelt neatly lettered 'J. PARRY TOWYN'. Here, too, he housed the many curious objects ranging from Chinese boxes to a model of the Statue of Liberty which he had either picked up himself when he was 'sailing foreign' or had presented to him more recently by fellow seamen who had not yet swallowed the anchor. John Parry, indeed, was a characteristic representative of the long and illustrious seafaring tradition of the Welsh coast, a tradition far too little known in England because it has been scarcely recorded in literature except by one classic book, *Immortal Sails*. On leaving the sea Mr Parry had turned his nimble fingers to model making and had produced among other things a very creditable model of a showman's traction engine which was exhibited in the window of the ironmonger's shop where he worked. If the railway wanted anything which the shop could not supply from stock, and our demands were numerous and varied, he spared no pains to get it for us in the shortest possible time. He was also adept at finding the right man to do odd out-of-the-way jobs for us such as cutting new cab spectacle glasses for the Corris engines. To us, working in a strange neighbourhood, such help was invaluable, while we could, moreover, always rely upon John Parry to lend an extra pair of very willing hands in an emergency.

Peter Williams occupied the little cottage adjoining the shed at Pendre which had been built for Bousted. He had spent many years of his life working at Bryn Eglwys and on the railway but had now retired to live at Pendre with his younger son and daughter-in-law. He was an old man of the most striking Welsh physical type, having a long narrow face, a great nose, and keen far-seeing eyes deep set under beetling brows. To these impressive features the lines of age and a luxuriant white moustache lent great character and dignity. With such a face, one felt, he should have been a Bard or an Arch Druid, though a benevolent one, for the wrinkles about his eyes were those of merriment. The old man was a mine of information about the past and possessed an inexhaustible store of anecdotes with which he would regale David and myself as he pottered about the loco shed. Too frail to do any heavy physical work, 'Old Peter', as we came to know him, none the less gave invaluable moral support by helping us to keep our sense of proportion in times of crisis in the motive power department. No railway disaster, however dire it might appear to us, would ever ruffle Peter's equanimity or cause him to betray any sign of surprise or concern. He had known the Talyllyn and its vagaries for far too long to be taken aback by anything which might happen. 'Oh bless you I've seen it happen many and many a time when old Jacob Rowlands was here. Yes indeed . . . aye, aye . . .' would be old Peter's typical rejoinder and the prelude to a long tale which, while David and I struggled in the engine pit beneath DOLGOCH, would at least remind us that we were by no means her first victims. His often repeated 'aye, aye,' pronounced slowly and philosophically and with a rising inflexion of the voice, was as characteristic of the man as was Mr Thomas's briskly interrogative 'Isn't it?' We looked upon Peter as an employee of the Company, for not only was he always willing to light up the locomotives for us in the morning provided the kindling was laid ready for him in the cab, but he was the self-appointed keeper of the railway's only protected crossing. A shrill scream from

DOLGOCH's whistle as she ran under Ty Mawr bridge on the down journey was the signal which brought him from his cottage to open the gates. And as he stood by to let her pass he would pull his watch out of his waistcoat pocket to check her time and reward punctuality with a 'Very good . . . very good . . . aye, aye.'

There were so many jobs crying out to be done on every side that it was difficult to decide where to begin. Indeed, with so few pairs of hands available, work always had to proceed on a system of priorities, first priority being the maintenance of one locomotive in working order and of a track fit for it to run upon. But although I much prefer practical to administrative work, it seemed to me on arrival that one first essential was to establish some form of order in the little office at the Wharf station which was, after all, the headquarters of the Company. Like everything else about the railway this room had remained firmly rooted in the Victorian age; it made no concession whatever to the twentieth century, was not in the best state of repair and looked as if it had not been spring-cleaned within living memory. One end of it had been fitted up as a booking office with a long counter, a ticket cabinet and a ticket date stamping machine. This last was of the early pattern on which a change of date type can only be affected with the aid of some pointed instrument such as a penknife, and where the ink ribbon must be periodically wound back by hand. It was thus to provide me with two of the hundred and one routine tasks which, when train services began, must be regularly attended to. In this case the penalty for failure to do so was to be forcibly brought home to me one busy August afternoon when the ribbon ran off its spool and as I struggled to thread it back again on its sinuous path round inaccessible corners I became only too painfully conscious of mounting impatience in the queue of potential passengers.

For the rest, the office furniture consisted of a long desk under the window of proportions suitable to the three high stools which seemed to anticipate a row of elderly clerks with quill pens; a knee-hole mahogany desk on a low dais; numerous shelves and a holograph copying press, and lastly no less than three safes, two of such size and weight that they had proved too heavy a burden for

'This room had remained firmly rooted in the Victorian age'. Edward Thomas in an arranged pose for *Picture Post* in 1949

'Change of date type can only be effected with the aid of some pointed instrument'. Ken Cope dispenses tickets for one and eight half returns to Abergynolwyn

'On one occasion she succeeded in trapping the Chief Mechanical Engineer in her "peculiar motion"'. On a happier occasion David Curwen introduces 'the old lady' to enthusiasts at Wharf

the rickety floor and threatened to sink through it into the foundations. Needless to say there was no telephone, while the only means of lighting was a duplex paraffin lamp with a bowl of opaque white glass. Over the windows, which had not been opened for years because the sash-cords had rotted away, there were faded blue blinds which did not work and from the chimney breast above the blackened cast iron grate a moon-faced clock with a broken mainspring looked down silently. On the higher and less accessible shelves lay a heavy blanket of black dust which must have been slowly thickening there since the day they were built. This aerial accumulation, as undisturbed, decade after decade, as the slow settlement of silt on a sea-bed, seemed symbolical of the railway's history, a history that had moved in a different time scale where fifty years had brought fewer changes than ten in our world. It was the same with the ledgers, the papers, the documents, maps and plans. They too seemed to have settled undisturbed layer by layer like the dust, so that to delve down into them was to journey back in imagination through the past as surely as a geologist cutting through a cross section of sedimentary rock. There, at the lowest level, was a copy of the original deposited Plans and Sections prepared by the engineer for submission to the Parliamentary Session of 1865, and a list of property holders along the route. There were copies of the original Staff Rules and of the Bye Laws, the latter bearing the stamp of approval of 'Her Majesty's Privy Council for Trade and Foreign Plantations'. There was a plan of the Extension of the railway from Abergynolwyn to Bryn Eglwys which bore in age-browned ink the bold signature 'J. Swinton Spooner, Civil Engineer'. There were many old time-tables of various dates and a store of copies of that early Guide Book to the railway to which I have already referred. There was a handsome gilt lettered pass entitling 'J.J. O'Sullivan, Esq., General Manager, Corris Rly.' to free travel on the Talyllyn during the year 1914. It was marked 'Available for all Stations' and signed H. Haydn Jones, Secretary and Manager. Among the bigger exhibits there was an old Clearing House map of the railways of the British Isles and a large scale plan of Bryn Eglwys Quarry showing the underground workings. On the railway map the Talyllyn was duly shown in distinctive colouring, but there were interesting gaps elsewhere. The Great Western Railway, for instance, was still the 'Great Way Round' with no cut-offs through Castle Cary or between Aynho and Ashenden, while the Great Central was still the provincial Manchester, Sheffield & Lincolnshire so that the name of Marylebone as yet possessed no railway significance. Much of the material concerned the slate trade rather than the railway; old tally books of stocks or sales; a Cambrian Railway postcard bearing a Victorian stamp addressed to the Aberdovey Slate and Slab Company, and what appeared to be a much earlier letter sent 'by bearer' to the same address from the master of a ship at Aberdovey concerning a cargo of slate. This was written in a beautiful copper-plate script but had been partially devoured by mice. There was a curious miscellany of objects also; a drawer full of tallow dips, presumably for issue to the quarrymen; an important looking key, doubtless the cause of some acute domestic crisis of long ago since it bore a label neatly inscribed: 'Found on seat, July, 1910'; some old packets of seeds as mummified as wheat from the tombs of the Pharaohs, and a tin of rat poison, partly used.

This catalogue will convey some idea of the quality of the collection but not of its quantity. The sorting out took some time because of the importance of preserving anything which could conceivably be of use or of historical interest, but eventually order was restored, or rather a new spaciousness achieved. Among the railway documents, one of the most useful discoveries was an old book of Share Certificates embossed with the Common Seal of the Company which none of us had ever seen before. It consisted of the Prince of Wales' feathers and the motto 'ICH DIEN' enclosed in a garter bearing the tile of the Company. I had no sooner set eyes on this than I pictured to myself how greatly the appearance of our locomotives would be enhanced if a suitably enlarged and coloured version of this seal could be emblazoned on bunker or cab sides in the brave tradition of the old railway companies. So I took a careful rubbing of the seal and sent it to our Secretary with my suggestion. He in turn passed it on to a keen member, at that time unknown to me who, as luck would have it, worked for a very old firm of transfer makers who had supplied in their day most of the early railway crests and coats of arms. The result was the very fine colour transfer which now adorns the Talyllyn locomotives.

In addition to these transfers, the locomotives were presented with handsome cast brass name and number plates. For it had been decided that the two Corris engines, which would retain their numbers three and four in our list, should be named SIR HAYDN and EDWARD THOMAS respectively. These locomotive embellishments were but two examples of the many contributions in kind which were now flowing in from individuals or commercial firms. These included a complete set of train lamps, new station name boards, station direction signs, glass-fronted cases for time-table display, poster boards and a plentiful supply of paint and varnish which stations, locomotives and rolling-stock alike all sorely needed.

One occasion of anxiety at this time was the visit of the Boiler Insurance Inspector to examine the boiler of DOLGOCH which David, at his request, had now completely stripped. While the Inspector went about his business, measuring the wastage of plates and seams and testing the firebox for deflection under hydraulic pressure, we awaited his verdict with as much anxiety as two parents awaiting a doctor's report on their sick child. When I state the undisputed but almost unbelievable fact that DOLGOCH still possesses her original boiler, which at this time was eighty-five years old, even the non-technically minded will be able to appreciate our trepidation. But to our unbounded relief the Inspector expressed himself agreeably surprised by the condition of the boiler and passed it for service at a working pressure of one hundred pounds per square inch. Undoubtedly part of the secret of this extraordinary longevity is that the boiler consists of a copper firebox, brass tubes and an outer box and barrel of Lowmoor iron, materials far less susceptible to the non-scaling but corrosive action of the soft, acidic moorland water. But the verdict was also a tribute to the memory of the vanished company of Cumbrian engineers who built her. No locomotive being built to-day will live so long.

I do not think that in calling this chronicle of the Talyllyn a railway adventure I have been guilty of exaggeration. For a small band of amateur railwaymen to undertake the operation of even the smoothest running of railways would have been venturesome enough, but one thing we soon learnt about the Talyllyn was that it never ran smoothly either in the figurative or the literal sense of the word. In its eccentric old age it seemed to have developed a waywardness of character which men who had grown old with it like Peter Williams might take for granted but which seldom failed to catch us unawares. For example, it was not for nothing that DOLGOCH soon earned the unofficial title of 'the old lady', for no ageing Prima Donna could be more temperamental. We were given a foretaste of things to come when, having lost no time in getting DOLGOCH ready for the road once more, David took her up the line on a trial trip. On this occasion she put on her best behaviour as though with the deliberate intention of beguiling her unsuspecting crew to take her as far as Dolgoch which they might not otherwise have done. For it was here that the unpleasant surprise was in store. The water tank was found to be completely dry; not a trickle of water was running in. Since DOLGOCH's water storage capacity is very limited and was already almost exhausted, what had begun as a pleasant evening excursion instantly became an occasion of crisis. David at once beat as rapid a retreat as the track permitted, not daring to add any more to the fire. It seemed highly probable that 'the old lady' would have to be ignominiously abandoned at some point along the line, but David just succeeded in coaxing her back to Pendre on less than twenty pounds of steam with a dead fire and the water out of sight in the bottom fitting of the gauge glass.

In our previous experience the tank at Dolgoch had always been full and overflowing, so that next evening we went up there to investigate the cause of the drought on this, the first occasion when we had needed the supply. The method of conducting water to the tank which we succeeded in tracing out proved to be of a simplicity typical of the Talyllyn. From the tank a pipe led straight up the mountainside to a small sump which, on lifting the heavy stone which covered it, also proved to be quite dry. But it was apparent that a second pipe fed this sump, and this we traced diagonally across the face of the mountain until it eventually seemed to disappear in the bed of a small stream. Further investigation, however, disclosed an old wooden beer barrel buried in the stream bed. Water flowed into this through a rectangular hole in the top, inadequately protected by a piece of wire netting, while the outlet pipe was situated half-way up one end. This arrangement left a generous sump in the bottom of the barrel, but we found that this had become filled above the level of the outlet with silt and gravel. When we had performed the dirty and damping operations of scooping out the contents of the barrel and clearing the pipe with a long length of fencing wire, water again began to flow into the tank. We also altered the course of the stream with stones and turves so as to ensure an adequate flow into the barrel in time of drought. I had expected that the operation of the Talyllyn would demand some versatility, but I little thought that I should so soon have to turn the experience gained by dabbling in and damming up mountain streams in early childhood to such practical account. Our work proved lastingly effective, too, for although there were occasional moments of anxiety when the flow dwindled, the Dolgoch water supply never again failed utterly.

It had always been the custom to open the railway for traffic during the Whitsun holiday. This year Whitsun fell in mid-May whereas we did not feel that regular running would prove economic until early June. Moreover, we wanted to give the permanent way workers 'total occupation' of the line east of Rhydyronen until the last possible moment. But because we were anxious to observe local custom as far as possible, it was decided to stage a formal opening of the line on Whit Monday by working a token shuttle service between Towyn and Rhydyronen on that day only. On his little press in Towyn Mr Basil Jones was commissioned to print a special announcement to this effect which was suitably displayed, and activity on the line quickened as the day approached. Whit Saturday saw an influx of volunteer helpers and for the first time that year a passenger train ran the length of the line carrying these volunteers and a van load of new signboards which were off-loaded as we went along. Sunday was mainly devoted to tidying and cleaning up operations. I had previously found time to give the red livery of the coaches a coat of varnish, and when the windows had been cleaned and the brass door handles polished the antiquated four-wheelers put the average modern main line train to shame in appearance, though not, it must be admitted, in comfort. The 'old lady', too, had been most carefully groomed and made up for the occasion. There had been no opportunity yet to repaint her completely or to add the new finery of brass name plates or transfers. But the judicious use of oily rags had made lustrous her old green coat, and like a dash of lipstick the fresh scarlet enamel on buffer beams which had previously been a sober black gave her a jaunty air of renewed youth which was no less effective for being superficial. The hand rail along the top of her boiler barrel, the balances of her safety valves, and even her cab spectacle frames which had hitherto been painted over, all had been polished till they shone like gold.

It would have been too bad if such careful preparation had been greeted by a day of rain, but fortunately for once the Welsh weather was kind on this eighty-fifth birthday of the Talyllyn, and all that Monday the sun shone down from a sky of cloudless blue.

In such weather it seemed that summer had arrived overnight. Mountains which had so recently looked sombre and brown under cloud now lay basking in a fresh green coat of newly unfolded bracken fronds, while every gorse bush was ablaze with a flame which rivalled the glittering brasswork of DOLGOCH as she slowly propelled her empty train down to the Wharf station. Here a sizeable crowd was awaiting her arrival, grouped about a station building which, with a newly painted name board and a red ensign floating from the mast that overtopped the roof ridge, looked as worthy of the occasion as the glittering train. Needless to day, the 'red duster' of the Mercantile Marine was Mr John Parry's special contribution to the festivities. It may not have been exactly appropriate to a railway station, but it certainly made a brave show as it fluttered in the light breeze against the bright blue sky.

Amongst the crowd were those whose efforts, in so many different directions, had helped to make this occasion possible, but

'The "red duster" of the Mercantile Marine was Mr John Parry's special contribution'. Bill Trinder cutting the tape for the Whitsun opening

John Adams

'"The old lady" had been most carefully groomed and made up for the occasion'. John Snell pulls out on DOLGOCH

The Times

'Next follow the three coaches by Marshalls of Birmingham'. The general manager sees a train of original stock out of Wharf station

The Times

'Amongst the crowd were those whose efforts, in so many different directions, had helped to make this occasion possible'. The inaugural Whit Sunday train turns round at Rhydyronen

The Times

the most important actors in the drama and the cynosure of every eye were the ancient locomotive and her train of four-wheelers. They will play the leading part in the pages which follow, so before the opening ceremony is performed and the first public service to be run by the new régime goes on its way, let us mingle with the crowd and examine them in greater detail.

Probably the first thing we notice about the train as a whole is that it is fitted with side buffers, a provision extremely rare on narrow gauge lines where the centre buffer-coupling is almost universal. Those on the locomotive are of out-of-scale size, wooden faced and with a pronounced and rather dispirited droop towards the rail. In appearance they seem only one remove from the leather-faced buffers fitted to stock of Liverpool & Manchester date. Scarlet coupling and connecting rods emphasise that phenomenal length of coupled wheel-base which gives DOLGOCH an improbable appearance reminiscent of the child's wooden toy of that elementary type in which any pretence of working verisimilitude is sacrificed to the constructional simplicity of fixing a wheel at each corner. But while the irreverent Philistine may smile at the combination of drooping buffers, curious wheel arrangement and tall, thin chimney, the more respectful and knowledgeable will observe that 'the old lady' possesses a pair of cylinders of remarkably large diameter and length of stroke for so small a locomotive. Herein lies the secret of the work she can perform on the low boiler pressure of a hundred pounds, and the reason why, even when she is steaming badly, she will go on pulling her train with a mere twenty-five pounds 'on the clock'. The drain cocks of these cylinders, like those of the valve chests, are not linked to any cab control but must be turned on and off individually, being but one example of the extreme functional simplicity which characterises the whole machine. Nor are there any frills. For example, the brass rail on the top of her boiler barrel, which appears to be merely a pleasing and rather Emett-like conceit, is provided for the vital purpose of enabling the unfortunate fireman to remain with his steed. For, when occasion demands, it is to this rail that he must cling with one hand while with the other he dribbles sand down the pipe of the engine's only sandbox on the nearside running plate. Between this rail and the large dome, from the side of which sprout two whistles of slightly different tone, there is an untidy, sizzling cluster of three steam stop valves. In theory, their function is to enable the steam supply to be cut off from the blower and the two injectors. On the side sheet of one bunker is the handsome oval brass plate which bears the maker's name and, in the centre in larger letters, the words FLETCHERS PATENT. If we peer beneath the boiler barrel we may see, hideously confined in the narrow space between the frames, that assemblage of rods and links which was part of this Patent and which Mr Edward Thomas once described as 'a Very Peculiar Motion'. Lastly, there is evidence of David's recent attention, notably the workmanlike mechanical lubricator on the offside running plate, and a new smoke-box door, this last a remarkable manufacturing feat in the primitive conditions prevailing at Pendre.

Inside her cab, DOLGOCH exhibits the same stark simplicity. Quite the most striking feature of this interior are the two long brass spring cases of the Salter safety valves which are mounted directly above the backplate of the firebox. If we are observant, we may notice that the scales on these columns show somewhat disparate readings, but that is the fault of the springs inside. The valves are in fact correctly loaded, for the needle of the pressure gauge directly above is pointing to the hundred mark and they are just beginning to lift. The controls for the two whistles, the blower and the steam valves of the two injectors project through holes in the cab weatherboard and the only fittings on the backplate itself are two try-cocks, a boiler filling plug, the water gauge (which David has wisely fitted with a protector) and the regulator. This last is of the old 'pull and push' type more commonly found on traction engines than locomotives. The art of driving 'the old lady' very largely consists in acquiring a judicious touch on this regulator for it not only has a lot of lost motion, but its action is apt to be 'all or nothing' if not treated with great respect. Moreover, with the locomotive at rest, there is an appreciable pause, while pressure is built up in the steam chests sufficient to hold the slide valves up to their faces, before the opening of the regulator is translated into forward motion. The 'old lady's' driver therefore has to humour her in much the same way that the driver of an old horse is content to give his steed a discreet flick with the reins and then wait for her to amble off at her own gait and in her own time. Woe betide him if this lack of instantaneous response should provoke him, either through inexperience or impatience, to give the regulator a second and sharper jerk! The effect of such peremptory treatment, sudden and violent, will forcibly remind him and, incidentally, every unfortunate passenger in the train, that age must not be treated in a manner so irreverent and peremptory.

This regulator is inclined to the off-side where the reversing lever is situated, for the engine is right-hand drive. Below the regulator and just above the firehole door is a small shelf on which stands warming an old teapot filled with cylinder oil. On the fireman's side is the pillar and handle of the screw brake which now works, thanks to David's ministrations. It applies shoes to the rear wheels only. The back of the cab, up to waist height, is occupied by the water tank which is filled through an elbow protruding through the back of the cab and stoppered by a large wooden bung. At each end of the tank are the handles controlling the water supply to the injectors. These last, mercifully, are not of the original Giffard type as still fitted on TALYLLYN but later replacements which work well. Unfortunately, however, they deliver through the original clack valves which, as we shall see, proved far from trouble free. Whereas the leading axle is carried on semi-elliptic springs, the trailing axle, sandwiched between water tank and firebox, perforce makes use of two pairs of volute springs which stand above the footplate for the unwary to trip over. This, then, is DOLGOCH, a steam locomotive reduced to the simplest terms. By the comparative standards of modern technics, any steam engine is a simple machine, but to anyone accustomed to 'the old lady's' footplate the cab of a Gresley or a Bulleid 'Pacific' looks as replete with controls as the cockpit of a multi-engined aircraft.

Coupled next to the engine is the one and only passenger coach which the Company possessed at the time of Captain Tyler's visit in 1866. It provides third class accommodation. Although it preceded the other coaches by only a small margin of time it is far more antiquated in appearance with its perfectly straight vertical sides which display their horizontal planking and a top window line set well below that of the roof. Unlike the rest of the coaching stock whose design and appearance manifestly anticipates, albeit crudely, the rolling-stock of to-day, this vehicle even in such details as door handles and springs with ornamental curlicues at the ends of their leaves, seems to hark back to its predecessors on the earliest railways and beyond them to the road coaches upon which they were modelled. Another characteristic distinguishing feature of this veteran is the large diameter of its wheels, a portion of which has to be enclosed in wheel arches beneath the seats. Because its springs have become tired with age and are apt to settle unduly beneath the weight of a full complement of passengers, this coach became known to us affectionately as 'Limping Lulu' and was always the first to be detached if the traffic was light.

Next follow the three coaches by Marshalls of Birmingham; one third class, one first/third composite and one first class. Although these distinctions of class have been retained, the train has operated on a 'third class only' basis since 1931 which means that the limited privilege of travelling 'first' falls to early arrivals. At different stages in their history the same coaches have provided first, second and third class accommodation and second and third class only. Externally all three are of identical construction with slightly curved sides smoothly panelled and roofs less flat than their predecessor. The single 'end first' compartment in the composite coach may once have been a smoking compartment before being elevated to first class, for there is a reference in railway records to a special smoking compartment which presumably marked the transition between the eras of complete prohibition and present-day toleration. It is completely insulated from the third class section of the carriage by a division, the only one in the train. Most probably, too, it was the only 'first' on the train during the brief period when three classes were catered for. Until holiday traffic grew to its present proportions and first class fares were abolished, the first class coach was seldom used and consequently it is in much better condition than the rest of the rolling-stock. The one compartment in the composite was usually sufficient to cater for the rare first class passengers and its most frequent occupant in the old days was the local doctor when he made periodical routine visits to the quarry at Bryn Eglwys. The livery of the first three coaches and the brake-van is a brick red picked out in brown, green and pale blue, but the first class coach, though lined out in the same fashion, wears a more sombre and dignified suit of maroon. It is apparent that this is an older livery which has survived on this coach because it spent so much of its life protected from the weather in the carriage shed. The coaches are lettered on the nearside only, and, for the reason explained in Captain Tyler's first report, all the doors on the offside of the train have been permanently secured, their handles removed and their drop windows barred. This has given rise to the often repeated legend that the coaches were built with doors upon one side only as an economy measure. Each coach consists of three compartments seating six passengers in what passes for comfort by Talyllyn standards, or eight in acute discomfort. The normal full complement of the train is therefore seventy-two persons but, as we shall see, this was often handsomely exceeded. The interiors are finished in scratch comb graining with ceilings of that white embossed paper known, I believe, as lincrusta. The unrelenting solidity of the hard wooden seats is mitigated only slightly in the first class compartments by thin, unsprung seat cushions and back rests covered in fawn bedford cord. The only other feature which distinguishes the first class accommodation are the notices requesting the passengers not to spit. Although I suspect that the other compartments once displayed similar injunctions which have since been painted out, the inference is that, as a kind of easement, the occupants of the hard seats may now expectorate without let or hindrance.

Finally, at the tail of the train we come to the brake-van. As old photographs show, this once possessed a look-out and double sliding doors on both sides, but first the doors and later the look-out on the offside were removed to leave no opening of any kind. At the end of the van nearest the train there is an external brake-screw and handle actuating wooden shoes on the wheels.

The Guard can work this brake through an end window fitted with a sliding shutter in the small booking office compartment which occupies one end. Wooden benches extend round three sides of the main body of the van to make a useful overflow when demand exceeds the normal supply of seats.

Such overflow accommodation was not required on this particular occasion until the later morning and afternoon. Nevertheless, there was a good muster of passengers who had come early to the scene to claim the distinction of having travelled on the first train of the season. When they were all aboard, Bill Trinder, as Chairman of the Society, made a short speech before ceremonially cutting a tape, which had been stretched across the track, and declaring the line open. His action was answered by a shrill blast of DOLGOCH's whistle and, punctual to the minute, the first service train to run under the new management drew out to the accompaniment of much excitement and acclamation.

A gang of volunteers was awaiting the arrival of the train at Rhydyronen for as there is no loop at this station the task of turning round involved man-handling the coaches. First the passengers were asked to disembark on to the platform, then the train was run back and held on the brakes while DOLGOCH was manoeuvred slowly and carefully over the points on to the disused dead-end siding. Once she was safely clear of the running line, everyone breathed a sigh of relief and proceeded to push the train past her and back into the platform. This procedure was repeated successfully throughout the day as trainload after trainload made the short journey up from Towyn.

At the Wharf station train movements were similarly handicapped by the lack of a loop, though here the steep gradient out of the station favoured the operation, for once the engine was safely in her siding the stock could be run back by gravity. This proved to be so much simpler than the old practice of propelling the train to and from the loop at Pendre that it became a regular practice throughout the summer, although it caused me a few moments of acute panic occasioned by an episode in the past which acted upon me like the Gypsy's Warning.

In the days when the slate trade prospered it became the custom for drivers to run round their loaded slate trains at Pendre and then propel them thence as far as the gradient down to the Wharf where they left the wagons standing on their brakes. This at once released the locomotive and at the same time meant that the men engaged in unloading and transhipping to standard gauge wagons on the Wharf could release the wagons as they required them and, with a hand on a brake lever, let them run into any of the several sidings. But on one fatal occasion a driver must have failed to secure the brakes effectually with the result that a rake of wagons loaded with slates, rapidly gaining momentum, shot through the station. Because the sidings end in wagon turntables and not buffer stops, the runaways ended their headlong career by leaping one after another off the edge of the Wharf and down on to the lines of the then Cambrian Railway like a file of frightened sheep leaping a ditch. The unfortunate driver responsible was promptly sacked, but he straightaway obtained employment on the Corris railway where he continued to drive for many years. What the Cambrian authorities had to say about the episode is not recorded.

This cautionary tale conjured in my imagination an all too vivid picture of the havoc which would ensue if our passenger stock were to follow a similarly suicidal course. My phobia was aggravated by the fact that our passenger brake was constructed in such a way that it was impossible to see, except at one particular angle and instant, whether the brake was manned or not. On more than one occasion when the coaches appeared to be lumbering down the gradient into the yard at more than their usual speed, I rushed out of the office prepared to make a desperate leap for the brake as they went by. But always, I am happy to say, a grimy hand would emerge from the dark interior and screw down the vital brake.

On the evening of that fine and successful Whit Monday the weighty matter of the summer time-table was discussed and decided upon at an informal meeting in the 'Corbett Arms'. For time was short, and a decision must be made so that an order could be placed with the local printer. There would be two booked trains in each direction per day as in the past, but on five days of the week, and the times would be altered to connect with main line services to and from Aberystwyth and Barmouth. Accordingly the morning service would leave the Wharf at 10.30 a.m. returning at 12.45 p.m., and the afternoon train at 2.45 p.m., returning at 5 p.m. In view of the state of the permanent way the overall journey time would be increased to an hour which meant a fifteen minute stand at Abergynolwyn between services. The previous afternoon departure time had been 2.15 p.m. and it was found that the alteration pleased the local people who, travelling into Towyn by the morning train, were allowed more time for shopping. The service would operate from Monday, June 4th until the end of September, leaving only Saturdays and Sundays clear so that the regular staff could draw breath and week-end parties of volunteer workers enjoy total occupation of the permanent way.

The next fortnight was one of the fullest of my life; for I was busy giving the woodwork and guttering at all stations a coat of fresh green paint; helping David in the shed; loading rails in a member's lorry at the foot of the incline at Abergynolwyn and transporting them to Brynglas where they were to be laid; dealing with the correspondence which flowed ceaselessly into the Wharf office and which often occupied me until far into the night; arranging the printing and distribution of time-tables, and last but not least, sorting out the many tickets which would now be required, for at Whitsun only Towyn to Rhydyronen tickets had been needed.

Beyond referring to the old ticket dating machine at the Wharf office, I have so far made no mention of the booking arrangements on the Talyllyn Railway, but at this point in the story some account and explanation becomes due. The railway has always issued Edmundson card tickets of orthodox type but with a preference for strong colours to distinguish the different issues. The earliest surviving specimens that I have seen have stencilled serial numbers and do not, unfortunately, show the fares. Yet they can scarcely have been lower than those prevailing in 1910 when a third class single from Towyn (Pendre) to Abergynolwyn cost 6½d. compared with the 1s. 6d. charged for the same journey in

1951. At one time, too, the single fare for a child from Towyn to Rhydyronen was 2¼d. Although I am no expert in this department of railway lore, I should imagine that halfpenny and farthing fares were unusual and that very few railways can ever have issued a card ticket for so small a fare as one halfpenny which, on the Talyllyn in 1910, would buy a third class half single from Rhydyronen to Brynglas.

The two original booking offices of the railway were at Pendre and Abergynolwyn, housed in two identical wooden station buildings. Of these the first still survives in its original condition, but the latter finally succumbed to wind and weather shortly before the Second World War and was replaced by a smaller stone building. To deal with intermediate station bookings, Mr Thomas's predecessor, R.B. Yates, was responsible for converting the Guard's compartment into a mobile ticket office. Racks were installed and the near-side look-out was fitted with a small counter, dating machine and issuing hatch. A similar contrivance once operated on the Glyn Valley Tramway, but with this exception the Talyllyn's office is unique. The two terminal booking offices may once have been regularly manned, but soon the Guard of the train became wholly responsible for booking and opened up these offices as required. The extension of passenger services to the Wharf station and the steady growth of tourist traffic which accompanied the decline of local trade meant that the new booking office at the Wharf accounted for the bulk of the traffic receipts and the volume of business done elsewhere shrank to negligible proportions. The two old booking offices were therefore closed and their business transferred to the van, but in the last years of the old régime even the van office was not used, and Mr Thomas merely collected money and issued no tickets to the few passengers who joined the train at any station other than the Wharf.

We had decided to bring our unique mobile booking office back into use. But despite the fact that most of the booking would be done at the Wharf and that we had decided to introduce paper tickets to cover some of the least popular intermediate journeys, the van would still have to carry a very wide range of tickets. In consequence our amateur guards were inclined to sympathise with Mr Thomas's policy of dispensing with tickets altogether when they found themselves faced with this most formidable display of tickets lodged in a space as dark and confined as a cupboard which reeled like a ship in a rough sea when the train was in motion, and where the only aid to the faint daylight was a bracket candlestick which had once seen service on a piano.

When we took over the working of the railway the tickets which we collected from these various offices, used or disused, were found to be so baffling in their number and confusion that it was decided to introduce new issues for many of the more popular bookings and to sell off most of the old ones, made up in assorted packets, to collectors or children. Hence I was faced with the task of sorting out a most bewildering miscellany of little bundles of tickets, mostly of new issue but some old and all, one hoped, numbered in sequence, and of arranging each in an appropriate rack either at the Wharf or in the van. As this was a department of railway operation of which I had had no previous experience or knowledge whatsoever, and as we did not number amongst our members any railway booking clerk to instruct me in the art, I had to proceed on the principle of trial and error until the procedure was mastered and became a matter of routine. In this, as in so many other ways, the Talyllyn Railway soon taught us that there is very much more involved in running even a small railway than driving or firing a locomotive, or blowing a whistle and waving a green flag. They are merely the more spectacular and public roles, and even they are not always such easy or enviable occupations as railway lovers of all ages are apt to suppose.

With little more than a week to go before regular running was due to begin there was a hitch. After a hard day spent moving rails I returned late one Saturday evening to the Wharf to find a telegram instructing me to suspend arrangements and not to display or circulate time-tables. So far as the latter were concerned the telegram came too late and before I could find out the reason for this disquieting message I had to wait, in considerable bewilderment and anxiety, until the following Monday morning. It then transpired that some members of our Committee had

'A space as dark and confined as a cupboard which reeled like a ship in a rough sea'. The mobile ticket office

The Times

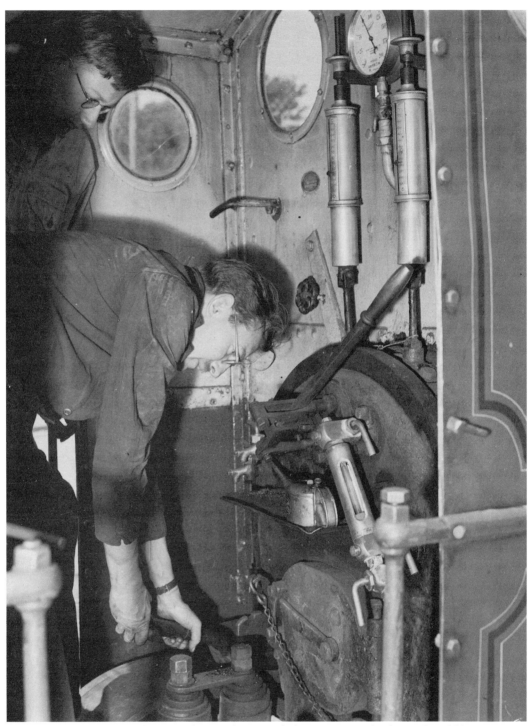

'The "old lady's" driver therefore has to humour her in much the same way as the driver of an old horse'. David Curwen and John Snell in the cab of DOLGOCH

The Times

decided that they could not accept their share of the responsibility involved in the decision to open the line to regular traffic throughout. Instead they had counselled running to Rhydyronen only, as we had done at Whitsun, and extending services from station to station up the valley as permanent way work progressed. Judged solely on engineering grounds there was weight in this argument, but from every other practical point of view it seemed to spell the doom of the whole venture. It would involve a great loss of traffic revenue, and this loss of money would mean that we might not be able to afford to undertake the necessary permanent way work at all. Moreover, there was no run round loop short of Abergynolwyn, while at Dolgoch there was not even a siding. So unless we could count upon constant volunteer help, or impress able-bodied passengers to push the coaches, it would be quite impossible to turn the train round at any intermediate station.

It was imperative that this last minute division of opinion as to the best policy to adopt should be settled without delay, and an emergency meeting was arranged in the Wharf station office. I was wholeheartedly in favour of running as we had originally planned in spite of the inevitable risks, because I could see no alternative but failure. Yet I now felt the responsibility of urging this very keenly. For I had been long enough at Towyn now to weigh the difficulties involved and I felt that the chances of running the season through without mishap or interruption were no better than even. But it was Mr Edward Thomas who, in the event, really clinched matters. I shall never forget his contribution to this eleventh hour meeting. It was characteristically brief and to the point. "I think you are taking things much too seriously, gentlemen," he said. "Let me tell you that if Lady Haydn had asked me to run the railway this year I should have run it without any of your help." So the Talyllyn Railway was given the green light and on Monday, June 4th, 1951, the summer service began.

Chapter Four

In the sunshine of the first Monday morning in June our railway adventure began in earnest when the first booked train for Abergynolwyn pulled away from Towyn. This time there were no enthusiastic crowds of well wishers to speed the train on its way, no ceremony and few passengers. But for the small permanent staff, for Dai Jones and John Snell on the footplate, for Bill Oliver who was in charge of the permanent way, and for David and myself, this was a momentous event. For us the much publicised festivities of Whitsun had been a brief honeymoon, whereas from this time forward until the summer's end we were bound by the inexorable daily routine of the time-table, and the railway's claim upon our lives would be complete and unremitting. No longer could to-day's job be completed to-morrow; the time-table imposed a new urgency and time became the inveterate arbiter and enemy. As though to emphasise this new situation, the clock in the Wharf station office, fitted with a new mainspring by one of our members, now ticked away the minutes with remorseless accuracy. It would receive many an anxious glance from me before the season was over.

Picture now the scene at the Wharf station on some bright morning of this month of June, and then in imagination let us ride the footplate of DOLGOCH as she hauls the ten-thirty up the valley to Abergynolwyn. On a wooden bench sheltered by rhododenron bushes covered with pink and purple blossom three old men are comfortably ensconced. They may possibly be prospective passengers, but it is much more likely that they have merely strolled down to watch the train go out. Not that the spectacle is any novelty to them because they have known the railway since they were boys, but it affords an excuse to enjoy the warmth of the sun, and to pass the time of day over a peaceful pipe. The murmur of their Welsh drifts lazily upon the air with the scent of their tobacco, and from where we stand they are half hidden from us by an enormous rounded boulder which lies close beside their seat. Incongruous in its isolation it might be a meteorite, but in fact it was brought down from the quarry many years ago as an impossibly weighty response to a request by a local lady for rockery stone and here it has lain ever since. Perhaps it 'seemed a mere pebble to those stalwart quarrymen of Bryn Eglwys.

About the doorway of the booking office there is a more animated group and an occasional thudding sound signifies that another ticket has been issued and stamped '15JUN51' on the old dating machine. Already some passengers have taken their seats in the waiting train. A gentle salt-laden breeze is blowing in from a sea which shows blue and sparkling above the rim of the green fields beyond the Wharf. It flutters the flag over the station building and plays with the smoke and the feather of steam that is drifting from DOLGOCH's chimney and safety valve. Her driver has been persuading some lubricant into the less accessible portions of the 'old lady's' 'peculiar motion' with the aid of a length of pipe, while the fireman goes from coach to coach pouring oil into the axle boxes from a pint bottle which once contained fizzy lemonade. These may be what are termed 'fat boxes' in theory, but grease does not melt till the bearings run warm whereas a little oil works wonders in reducing rolling resistance. But now both the driver and the fireman have climbed back on to the footplate and it is time we joined them there. For the stationmaster-cum-booking-clerk had locked up the station office and has now assumed the role of guard. He checks all carriage doors to see that they are properly shut, screws off the brake in his van and then gives us the 'right away' which we acknowledge on the whistle. Our driver then moves his reversing lever into forward gear and persuasively joggles the handle of the regulator to and fro until we can hear a faint sound of steam escaping punctuated by a just audible click as the valves come up and we start to move forward. DOLGOCH does not advertise her departure by any sharp staccato bark such as her large but youthful neighbours on the main line effect. So vigorous and vocal a display of power would be unseemly and even vulgar at her age. Instead there emerges from her tall thin chimney a decorous but slightly uneven and breathless panting sound which strengthens and deepens to a hoarse and throaty roar as she exerts her maximum effort on the steep gradient up the cutting beyond the Wharf bridge. The gradient is short, and the regulator is first eased and then closed as we enter the straight run on a slightly falling gradient into Pendre station. Ahead we can see old Peter opening the crossing gates in answer to our warning whistle, and as we run over the points which lead off to the loop and the shed roads, DOLGOCH rolls alarmingly like a ship encountering a sudden heavy sea on the beam. So early in the season it is unlikely that there will be any passengers for this morning train at Pendre, but we make a brief routine stop, passing the time of day with Peter and exchanging a word with David who, wiping his hands on a piece of cotton waste, has come out of the shed to see us go through.

The gradients on the Talyllyn Railway are deceptive. The passenger is not unnaturally led to suppose that the climbing is done on the upper section between Brynglas and Abergynolwyn where the line clings to its narrow shelf high above the valley floor. Yet in point of fact the heaviest locomotive work is performed on the first unspectacular section between Towyn and Rhydyronen where the high, overgrown hedges which brush the sides of the coaches conceal the fact that the line is rapidly gaining height. As DOLGOCH again starts to labour heavily we learn that this ascent begins on the first curve east of Pendre, stiffens as we approach the first overbridge called Ty Mawr, and continues with unrelenting severity until we have gained the next bridge past Hen-dy farm. Here 'the old lady', a little breathless by this time as the pressure gauge shows, can be eased somewhat until she has traversed the dog-leg curves beyond the gateway which is Fach Goch halt. The second of these curves brings us on to the relaid 'Corris straight', a long climb at 1 in 60 whose summit is marked by Cynfal bridge and platform. But with this newly laid rail under her wheels, DOLGOCH roars up this bank in fine style to demonstrate what a handsome slice she could cut from the

'Monday, June 4th, 1951, the summer service began'

'There emerges from her tall thin chimney a decorous but slightly uneven and breathless panting sound.' DOLGOCH leaves Wharf on a time-tabled train in 1949

B.R. Photographic

'DOLGOCH starts to labour heavily . . . stiffens as we approach the first overbridge called Ty Mawr.' John Snell drives No. 2 at Hendy Bridge in 1951

T.R. Archive

running schedule, even at her age, if only the track was in this condition throughout. But alas, this 'galloping ground' is all too limited as yet. It is followed by a very short length which was relaid in Sir Haydn's day with rails purchased from the dismantled Glyn Valley Tramway, but then we are back on the old road again, and as we look ahead at the line of rails, wavering, tenuous, in places hardly visible in the grass, it looks scarcely capable of supporting the passage of an empty wagon let alone our eight ton locomotive. Fortunately for the average passenger's peace of mind the old coaches ride remarkably well all things considered, but no one who has ridden the footplate of DOLGOCH can harbour any illusions about the state of the permanent way. The engine rolls and snakes along on the uneven way, rough rail joints bring a series of sickening jolts and crashes, while it is disconcerting to look ahead and see an occasional loose rail leaping up as it receives our weight. To experience this is to marvel at the fact that our old locomotive has not shaken herself to pieces irreparably years ago.

Although officially, according to Captain Tyler's report, the steepest gradient on the line is 1 in 60, it is generally believed that the short, vicious little bank out of Rhydyronen station is the worst on the railway and nearer 1 in 40 than 1 in 60. Conditions conspire to make it as awkward as can be. A stop at Rhydyronen means that it has to be tackled from a standing start; it is upon a curve, and the rail is often greasy by reason of the hedges and trees which shade the line at this point. On this occasion the guard has advised the loco crew that we have no passengers on board for Rhydyronen, and as there is no sign of life on the little platform we run through the station and, with our flying start, surmount the incline without any difficulty. Curiously enough the summit of this gradient is a bridge over the Braich-y-Rhiw stream beyond which the line falls away quite steeply for about 200 yards. This is the only notable favouring gradient which an up-train encounters between Pendre and Abergynolwyn, and it was here in the old days that picnic parties, bowling back to Towyn in their hired wagons, were apt to find some manual assistance necessary. From the foot of this short decline we begin to climb once more, not so steeply but steadily, all the way to Brynglas, where, after a warning whistle for the unprotected crossing, we draw up at the small ivy covered station. Maybe there are no passengers to pick up, but having run through Rhydyronen we are ahead of schedule and the pause will give DOLGOCH, at the best of times rather a tricky steamer, a chance to recover her breath for the long pull of nearly two miles to Dolgoch.

With the needle of the pressure gauge almost back to the hundred mark we draw out of Brynglas and into the long cutting which soon became known to us as 'Tadpole' because, as a result of the choked ditches, heavy rain often floods the road bed here above rail level. From this cutting onwards the uneasy motion of our locomotive, an oscillation not merely vertical, as Captain Tyler described it, but in every other direction, becomes more disquieting, especially as we are standing on the left-hand side of the footplate. For we have reached the spectacular part of the journey and for almost the whole of the way from here to Abergynolwyn the ground falls away steeply on this side of the line. As we approach the Dolgoch viaduct the road ahead looks more like a grassy woodland ride than a railway, and that we should be following such a path on the footplate of a locomotive seems almost as unbelievable as a fairy story. There is indeed an element of fantasy about the Talyllyn. In any surroundings this ancient train which has travelled straight out of the mid-Victorian era would look strange enough, but its appearance in this setting of wild landscape seems too improbable to be true. An unexpected glimpse, either from the floor of the valley below or from the heights above, of DOLGOCH and her train of box-like four-wheelers creeping along the mountain sides under a tell-tale banner of white steam, and reduced to the size of a toy by the scale of the scenery, is enough to make a stranger rub his eyes and believe that, even in this stereotyped and materialistic century, the age of miracles is not past. It is equally remarkable to stand at Dolgoch when the trees on the slopes in their high summer foliage conceal the line from view, and to hear, high above, the improbable sound of a locomotive whistle, followed by an extraordinary, syncopated but quite unrhythmical, clank and clatter as our train runs over the viaduct and into the station.

At Dolgoch our driver is at pains to bring 'the old lady' to a stand precisely opposite the water column, a feat which calls for no mean skill and which even after long experience sometimes fails to come off. The fireman then lifts the wooden bung out of the tank filler and lowers into position the wooden chute which, when not in use, slides back into a recess in the stone pillar beneath the wooden supply tank. The driver then pulls the wire which, via a pivoted lever, lifts the crude wooden flap valve and sends a torrent of water gushing down the trough, some of it to enter the tank but much more to wash the rear buffers. By now this simple operation must have been recorded in thousands of photograph albums throughout the length and breadth of Britain. For most of the passengers get out of the train at this point even if they are travelling through to Abergynolwyn, and the combination of DOLGOCH, the water column, the work in hand and the station in its setting of rhododendron bushes and encircling mountains appears to be irresistibly photogenic. Out come the cameras, from the railway enthusiast's expensive Leica or Contax to young Johnnie's box Brownie with its spool of holiday 'snaps', and the clicking of shutters sounds like the stridulation of grasshoppers or the bursting of seed pods in a summer meadow. No film star can have been more frequently photographed than 'the old lady', so no wonder she is inclined to be temperamental.

When the tank has been filled and the guard has told the last passenger the way to the waterfalls we start away on the last lap. Though the scenery here is wilder, this final stage of the journey is easier than what has gone before. At Quarry siding the hard work is over, for the long straight stretches between the siding and Abergynolwyn, though still inclining upwards, are very easily graded. Leaving the bare mountain side for the shelter of a belt of stunted oak trees, the little platform of the terminus soon comes into sight ahead and in a few moments we clatter over the points of the loop and come to a stand. We are on time. The guard screws down his van brake, the fireman uncouples and DOLGOCH runs round her train. Her labours are ended for the morning, for except on that short bank near Rhydyronen she will need very little steam to take her train back to Towyn.

Whereas good running on the up journey depends a great deal on the skill of the fireman, regular running on the falling gradient calls for more skill on the driver's part in handling that tricky regulator combined with a good working knowledge of the road. Though the gradient is seldom or never steep enough for speed to be maintained for long with steam shut off, anything more than a whiff of steam will at once produce excessive speed so that, with a heavy hand on the regulator, progress is prone to alternate continually and disconcertingly between the too slow and the too fast.

In the narrow upper valley between Dolgoch and Abergynolwyn, road and rail run closely parallel, the road at a lower level in the valley bottom. Consequently, although these two upper stations account for at least ninety per cent of the tourist traffic, local trade is almost non-existent because of the proximity of the competing bus route. But at Brynglas, Rhydyronen and the two halts the position is reversed, for below Dolgoch the road and rail take opposite sides of the broadening valley, diverging until they are a long half mile apart. So, particularly if it is Friday, which is the most favoured shopping day, we shall be on the look out for passengers at the two lower stations, on the little platform under the hedge at Cynfal and in the gateway at Fach Goch.

Although from a revenue point of view this local traffic is negligible and it is upon the patronage of the holiday maker that the railway has to depend for its bread and butter, we of the small permanent staff attached the greatest importance to it and did our utmost to ensure that, whatever else might happen, we should not let our regular passengers down. For the Talyllyn Railway was not built, like a miniature railway on a sea-front, as a side show for tourists, but for two practical purposes, both intimately linked with the workaday life of the district. Firstly it was built to carry slate from the quarry, secondly it was intended to serve the needs of the scattered Welsh community in its mountain valley. The first function had, alas, gone beyond recall, but I was determined that so long as one local passenger remained the railway should continue to fulfil, to the best of our ability, the motto 'ICH DIEN' which it proudly bore upon its crest, and I came to look upon the tourist traffic as an essential means to this end. To be able to give pleasure to thousands of holiday makers, as the railway undoubtedly does, is very gratifying, particularly in these drab days, but it is not service. It is very enjoyable for the Smith family from Manchester to travel up to Dolgoch to spend an hour exploring the waterfalls and we must do our best not to disappoint them and to see that they are carried punctually. But their journey is part of an interlude in a life spent in a remote city in which the railway plays no part. The Smith family are here to-day and gone to-morrow, but the Joneses, the Evanses and the Pughes are with us always. Better that the Smiths should miss their excursion to the waterfalls than that Mrs Jones with her heavy baskets should wait in vain, or Mr Pugh fail to receive his sacks of pig-meal.

To allow the money in the visitor's pocket to outweigh local needs would be as fatal for us as it would be for a farmer with a houseful of summer guests to leave his sheep to rot upon his mountain. For at once railway and farm alike would fall out of the historical and regional context of which they have so long been a part and in which alone they have their true being. This is the great danger of the growth of 'tourism' in Wales, and the more dependent the Welsh become on the summer visitor the greater grows the risk that an ancient birthright will be squandered for the proverbial mess of potage. For Wales is not merely a landscape of mountain and waterfall and beach, a convenient empty space on the map where the population of our swollen cities can find a breathing space. Nor is it a no man's land to be covered by a regimented forest of conifers, flooded by new reservoirs or blasted by high explosive weapons. Wales is the ages old association of people with landscape in an ecological partnership intimately interlinked. To the landscape the people have given the sheep, the black cattle and the small hill farms; the dry-stone boundary walls and moutain quarries; the little market towns and sea-ports. To the people the mountains have given a way of life and, until the twentieth-century invasion, they have nursed and protected the language and the traditions of a people which are the expression of that way of life. But these mountain dykes are down now. Every summer a tide of tourists, each stronger than the last, spills over them to flood Wales just as surely and inevitably as successive tides battered down those sea walls that the drunken Seithenyn so slothfully failed to guard and so drowned the lost kingdom under Cardigan Bay.

That the Welsh language should survive as strongly as it does in this part of Mid-Wales is a tribute to the strength and vigour of the native tradition, but the price of invasion is patently apparent in sprawling coastal towns, in military camps, in battalions of conifers, in breached walls, ruined farms and abandoned quarries. Though I had come over the mountains as an invader myself, I felt that a childhood spent at Welsh Hay gave me some sort of passport, and before long I found myself looking at the summer invasion from the Welshman's point of view. At the height of the holiday season our little train symbolised the whole situation. The four coaches would be so packed out by tourists, so resonant with the loud, harsh accents of London, Lancashire, Birmingham or the Black Country, that I would ask the locals to travel with me in the van. Their soft Welsh voices, quiet good manners, and a friend-liness which made me feel one of themselves were at once a tonic and a contrast. On such occasions it was as though our brake-van had become the last stubbornly held strong point for a local underground resistance movement forced to take desperate defen-sive measures. But when the invaders retreated with the coming of autumn, local life would reassert itself. So far as we were concerned its beleaguered forces would soon take the offensive and advance to reoccupy their old well chosen positions in the first class coach.

As is natural where so few surnames are divided among so many, we soon learnt to refer to the individual members of this little band by surname coupled to that of their native place in the Welsh fashion thus: Mr Jones Pandy Mill, Mrs Jones Llwynwcws, Mrs Evans Caerffynnon, Miss Roberts Cynfal. We are looking out for them now on our journey back to Towyn; for the two unrelated members of the Jones clan at Brynglas and for Mrs Evans at Rydyronen where she may be accompanied by several others including, perhaps, old Mr Pugh with his white stick and his wireless battery. Mr Pugh was a platelayer on the railway for

'A glimpse from the heights above. DOLGOCH and her train of box-like four-wheelers creeping along the mountain'. A general view looking up to the head of the valley

The Hulton Deutsch Collection

'The improbable sound of a locomotive whistle . . . syncopated but quite unrhythmical clank and clatter'. DOLGOCH runs over the viaduct in 1951

P.B. Whitehouse

'We are on time'. The train at Abergynolwyn in 1951

P.B. Whitehouse

very many years until his sight failed, and in recognition of this long service he has been rewarded with honorary membership of the Society which allows him to travel free. He is one of the few 'regulars' who sometimes travels with us to Dolgoch, for he occasionally visits his married daughter there. He is a heavily built old man of nearly eighty years and he is almost totally blind; but he is very active and has known the railway for far too many years to experience any difficulty in getting in and out of the coaches or the van.

With the last local passenger safely on board we are soon rattling under Ty Mawr bridge with a piercing whistle as a signal to old Peter to open the crossing for us. In spite of the additional stops we are on time when we pull up at Pendre, for the same timing of an hour for the down journey gives us a comfortable margin. Exept on the rare occasions when they intend catching a main line connection to Barmouth, Machynlleth or further afield, the locals will leave us at Pendre because this station is handier for the shops at the top of the town. They will work their way down through the town and catch the afternoon train back from the Wharf terminus. So we are a holiday train once more as we move off on the final short section through the cutting. Our fireman screws down the brake on the last steep gradient, and we run cautiously under the bridge and over the points to draw up in the Wharf station yard. The hands of the office clock show 12.45, and 'the old lady' has added yet another to her score of many thousand journeys.

With the object of conveying to the reader the impression of the railway which the vast majority of our passengers gained, I have deliberately described a typical journey when everything has gone well and time-keeping has been exemplary. But if the railway had always run so smoothly this book would scarcely merit its title, nor would the enterprise have been so well worth while. For, to use a phrase of the poet W.B. Yeats, there is such a thing as 'the fascination of what's difficult'. That we were enthusiasts indulging our love of railways in general and the Talyllyn in particular is true, but the appetite soon sickens of the fruits of any form of self-indulgence unless they come as a reward for hard labour and difficulties overcome. There was certainly no lack of difficulties, often of a most exasperating kind, on the Talyllyn, but looking back upon the experiences of this first season I realise that its most rewarding moments were not the periods of calm (for the longer they lasted the stronger became the conviction of impending disaster) but the occasions when we succeeded in maintaining the service against all the bounds of human or mechanical probability.

Excluding the occasional extra evening trains which we ran for special parties, there were ten round trips to be made weekly, and I would estimate that on the average in each week there was one trip on which there was trouble of one sort or another. But to maintain the service, even on the trouble free days, involved much more organisation, forethought and unobtrusive work than the ordinary passenger ever realised. This was particularly true of the locomotive department.

The steam locomotive is not only one of the simplest machines for its purpose ever devised; no other machine is capable of such reliability over so long a period of years. But as the price of this simplicity and reliability it exacts eternal vigilance and skill from those responsible for maintaining and operating it. One discovery I made in the course of this Talyllyn adventure was that some railway enthusiasts could display a positively encyclopaedic knowledge of locomotive history, of classes, builders and numbers, of all of which I was abysmally ignorant, and yet appear quite unable or unwilling to grasp the mundane but essential practicalities of the machines they were studying. They seemed to equate locomotive maintenance with that of the average motor-car where it is sufficient to send it to the garage for a routine overhaul every so many thousand miles. This is a completely false analogy. Even the most modern of locomotives requires constant attention. Apart from the obvious need to keep her supplied with coal, water, sand and lubricants of the right quality there are the tubes to sweep, the smoke-box to empty and glands and lubricator trimmings which require frequent adjustment, repacking or renewal. But in addition, DOLGOCH was no modern locomotive but one of the oldest in service in the world and a machine constantly racked by the rough track on which she had to run. In this matter of maintenance, therefore, to draw a parallel which will give any adequate idea of what keeping DOLGOCH in service involved we should have to imagine the owner of some 'horseless carriage' built at the turn of the century using his vehicle daily in the course of his business over a road consisting of an interminable succession of pot-holes.

The sun which had greeted us so benignly at Whitsun and on the first day of the summer service could not shine for ever, particularly in West Wales, and we very soon learnt that one of our worst enemies was the weather. A heavy downpour was not too bad because it rapidly washed the rail clean. The kind of weather which really spelt trouble on the Talyllyn was that which the Irish describe as a 'soft day'; a day when clouds hung low on the mountains and when there fell from them a continual dew. Too damp for mist, too thin for rain, it beaded every grass blade with droplets so gentle was its fall, but under such grey skies there was no sparkle as of morning dew or frost, only a sad lack-lustre sheen like unpolished silver on every tree and hedge and sloping field. It was this very gentleness which proved our undoing, for instead of washing our rails clean, the moisture combined with the fine powder of rust upon their running surface in an oily amalgam so slippery that, with a heavy rain behind her, the 'old lady's' ascent to Abergynolwyn became as difficult a feat as climbing a greasy pole.

The inadequacy of our sanding arrangements made matters much worse. There were no facilities for drying or storing sand at Pendre Shed, so to replenish our sand-boxes we had to make periodic visits to Towyn beach armed with all the buckets we could muster, with spades and a sheet of perforated zinc through which to sieve the sand. Holiday makers were apt to look somewhat askance at these bucket-and-spade activities on the part of grown, and often very grimy men. If the sand was not perfectly dry we would then have to rig up a primitive dryer consisting of a metal tray supported on firebricks over the smith's hearth in the repair shop. Then DOLGOCH's primitive sanding gear was far from efficient. The pipe from the sand-box was so arranged that most of the sand went anywhere but on to the running surface where it was needed. Bitter experience soon drove us to cure this trouble, but there remained the disadvantage that only one rail was sanded.

Whenever these weather conditions occurred, and that was not seldom, it became a desperate struggle to get the train up to Abergynolwyn. But, barring mechanical failure of which more anon, we never once failed to get there although we sometimes dropped as much as half an hour on schedule. Sometimes it seemed as though a hostile clerk of the weather was diabolically determined to catch us unprepared, for often this damnable damping would come on just as the train was due to leave Towyn. Then, as soon as we reached the first steep gradient at Ty Mawr our troubles would begin. We would creep as far as the curve just beyond the bridge and then stall, sometimes not merely coming to a stand, but sliding back with the weight of the train. The climb from this point up to the next bridge at Hendy, and Cynfal bank were the greatest obstacles under these conditions, and once they had been surmounted we considered the battle more than half won. Rhydyronen bank, though steeper, was so short that it was not so formidable, and if the train stopped at Rhydyronen we sometimes ran ahead while the train was at the platform, sanding the rail to the top of the bank with the aid of a watering can.

This watering can and a bucket, both filled with sand, were kept in the van in case of emergency. When acting as guard, which I did almost invariably throughout this first season, I had sometimes to leave my post in charge of a deputy and go forward to help the engine crew. While the fireman crouched on the running plate to operate the sand-box, I would perch precariously on the offside of the front buffer beam with watering can in hand and pour sand on to the other rail. I have ridden in this way from the bottom of Cynfal bank to Abergynolwyn and arrived soaked to the skin except for a small portion of my anatomy which was nearly roasted from too close a proximity to a hot smoke-box door. It is not a method of travel to be recommended at any time, let alone on a wet day. I recall another occasion when Bill Oliver and I dropped unobtrusively out of the van near Ty Mawr and pushed up behind until we were breathless. This may sound as futile as

No. 3 raising steam for the first time assisted by Bill Harvey, the general manager, and Bill Oliver looking on

John Snell

'The method of getting water to the boiler'. No. 3, SIR HAYDN, with David Curwen and Tom Rolt at Dolgoch on her first trip

John Snell

No. 3's trial run. The exhausted attenders pose on their return to Pendre for John Snell. Left to right: Tom Rolt, David Curwen and Allan Garraway

Gareth Jones drives SIR HAYDYN over relaid track and past the reconstituted water supply at Pendre, in place of the 'large wooden water tank, supported on a framework of old rails'.

John Adams

attempting to fend off an ocean liner with a punt pole, but in fact it was surprising how even the very limited help of two man-power could prevent DOLGOCH from stalling. On all such occasions of stress I endeavoured to avoid attracting the attention of passengers to what was afoot. This was partly a question of upholding Talyllyn prestige by giving and showing no cause for concern. But it was also to avoid becoming a target for facetious jokes. What motorist has not, when struggling to change a wheel by the roadside, been seized with an almost uncontrollable desire to strangle that inescapable small boy who always appears from nowhere with the question 'Got a puncture, mister?' The effect upon us in moments of stress of such remarks as 'What's up, chum, has she gone off the boil?' or 'Is this where we start to walk?' was very similar and strained almost to breaking point our rule of courtesy to the travelling public. But it is only fair to add that the great majority of our many passengers showed great consideration and good humour in such circumstances.

A good example of this forbearance was the occasion of our first serious mechanical breakdown which was caused by the stresses set up through violent slipping on a greasy rail. The day had started badly, for John Snell had been taken ill and we were therefore without a fireman. We were very shorthanded and I was particularly anxious not to take David away from his work on Corris No. 3 at Pendre. But I was fortunate enough to obtain the services of a very efficient relief guard and this enabled me to take John's place as fireman to Dai Jones. On the morning run everything went smoothly, but in the afternoon there was a baleful light shower of rain just before we were due to start out with a full train of four coaches. We had to fight for adhesion all the way to Rhydyronen and I had been sanding constantly. But now we were well on the way to Brynglas and though I was still sanding, the worst grades were behind us, and the rail was drying rapidly. I was just congratulating myself that another battle had been won when I heard DOLGOCH's exhaust beat suddenly change. It became progressively more uneven, then she lost a beat altogether and finally after a few yards of labouring progress she came to a stop. In a few bewildering moments our first real crisis was upon us. Here we were, with a trainload of passengers, many of whom had to catch rail connections back to Barmouth or Aberdovey, stuck on that very part of the line which was furthest from the road. There was, of course, time for them to walk back down the line, but I was determined to avoid this ignominious blot on our prestige if it was humanly possible. It was quite obvious that Mr Fletcher's Patent valve motion had become seriously deranged in some way or other, but without losing time on investigation I sent the guard post haste on foot up the line to Brynglas. I knew that Bill Oliver was at work there and that he must at once drive to Pendre in his van to fetch David and a kit of tools. By the time David joined me, and the operation was carried out very speedily, I had discovered that the nearside forward eccentric strap appeared to have seized on its sheave, though why it should have done so I could not conceive because one of our causes of concern had been the undue amount of play between these two components. In order to appreciate our predicament I must again stress the inaccessibility of this inside valve motion. Short of digging a pit between the rails under the engine it was difficult enough to examine it closely let alone to work on it. After a brief consultation we decided that the only thing we could do on the spot would be to try to take down the motion on the near side in the hope that DOLGOCH would be capable of moving 'on one side', that is to say on the offside cylinder only. Lying on our backs in the wet grass we succeeded after some difficulty in doing this, tying up the free ends of the rods to one of the boiler lagging bands with a piece of wire and locking the valve in mid-position by screwing up the spindle gland nuts dead tight. Fortunately by this time the rail had dried and this gave 'the old lady' a fair chance to perform what I shall always consider to be the greatest feat of her long lifetime. This was to haul her loaded train of four coaches and the van up the half-mile of rising gradient to Brynglas on one cylinder only. Here I had decided to follow the procedure we had adopted at Rhydyronen at Whitsun. DOLGOCH was uncoupled and run on to the siding and, with the willing help of some of the passengers, the train was then pushed past her. Having succeeded in hauling her train up to Brynglas it was obvious that, barring

90

some further disaster, she would run back to Towyn without difficulty, and so it proved. Actually we ran into the Wharf terminus not far behind scheduled time so that a casual passer-by would not have guessed that anything had been amiss. Throughout the whole trying afternoon our passengers had displayed exemplary patience and good humour and when, on our return, I offered a refund on the unexpired portion of their tickets, not one came forward to claim it although all had booked either to Dolgoch or to Abergynolwyn. So far from being disgruntled, several said they had enjoyed the adventure and expressed admir-ation for the way we had dealt with the situation and brought the train back when they had thought that a long walk was inevitable.

Meanwhile David lost no time in getting the engine back to shed and over the pit so that he could hold an inquest on the disaster, and as soon as I had counted the day's takings and balanced the books at the Wharf, I joined him there. What had happened was that sudden violent slipping and the inertia of the eccentric had caused one of the cotters (which secure the pins holding the two halves of the eccentric sheave together on the axle) to loosen and fall out. The two halves of the sheave had then opened slightly, over-ridden the axle key and jammed in the eccentric strap. Thus the immediate cause of the disaster had been the lost of a cotter measuring only about one and a half inches long, less than an inch wide and an eighth of an inch thick. It was indeed the locomotive equivalent of the proverbial loose nail in the shoe of the courier's horse which led to the loss of a battle. By the time a new cotter had been made and fitted and the valve gear reassembled it was late, for the offending eccentric was devilishly inaccessible, and we were working in the smoky, flickering light of tallow dips filched from that drawer in the Wharf office. But we locked up the shed and went home that night with the gratifying knowledge that DOLGOCH was ready for the morning train.

It was not very long after this incident that disaster struck again with even more startling suddenness and with consequences more serious both to prestige and to traffic revenue. It had been a fine morning and DOLGOCH was just running into Pendre station on her down journey after an uneventful trip when, with an alarming crash followed by a tinkling sound, she suddenly vomited a shower of broken spring leaves on to the 'two foot'. Her nearside front spring had completed disintegrated. On this occasion our passengers remained blissfully unaware of the consternation which instantly prevailed in the motive power department, for we pulled up in the platform at Pendre as though nothing had happened and after a brief whispered debate decided to run on to the Wharf as usual. It was only when the last passenger was safely out of sight that we set to work to get our crippled engine back to shed. This was not easy, for she had acquired so forlorn a list to port that the leading driving wheel on that side was bearing heavily against the frame. Moreover it was not just a question of moving herself; before she was free to run light to Pendre the train had to be pushed back up the incline. However, with manual assistance this operation was successfully completed. Once we had got DOLGOCH into the shed we no longer felt unduly concerned. We had luckily unearthed a spare spring in the repair shop and, on the average locomotive, changing a spring is not a very formid- able operation as locomotive repairs go. If we sacrificed our lunch we should have her ready in time for the 2.45 train. Alas for such complacency! As we very soon discovered and should by now have realised, DOLGOCH is by no means an average locomotive.

Working in the engine pit beneath DOLGOCH is not only the dirtiest but also the most temper trying job imaginable. No locomotive was ever more aptly assigned the feminine gender for no piece of machinery could be at once so endearing and yet so fickle and at times so exasperating. If she ailed it usually seemed to be in some part of her anatomy so inaccessible as almost to defy treatment. Moreover, whichever spanner her hapless surgeon picked up was always the wrong one, for most of the nuts and bolts which held her together were not only of sizes unknown to Mr Whitworth but differed one from another and individually across their flats. She was, too, an extremely difficult patient, expressing her resentment by transforming herself into a very fair imitation of some medieval engine of torture. Thus on one occasion she succeeded in trapping the Chief Mechanical Engineer himself in her 'peculiar motion' in such a close and deadly embrace that he was unable to move and scarcely able to breathe. David had been working in the pit with both arms above his head when one of the eccentric rods which he had detached at one end swung down and pinioned him in such a way that he was quite unable to free himself. Had he been working alone the sequel might not have been at all funny, but fortunately he was able to call for help to John Snell who happened to be in the adjoining repair shop at the time. Working under DOLGOCH while she was in steam, as we were on this occasion of the broken spring, added extreme heat to the burden of discomfort and greatly extended her capacity for mischief. Thus she was adept at directing thin jets of scalding water down the back of one's neck at a crucial stage in the proceedings or, since she possessed no ash pan, subjecting any unfortunate who passed beneath her firebox to a sudden rain of red hot cinders.

It was under these conditions that, with the sweat rolling off us, we struggled throughout the lunch hour to fit the replacement spring. I will not burden the reader with technicalities except to say that we soon came to the conclusion that on that far-off day when Mr Fletcher and Mr Jennings commenced to erect their patent locomotive they must have begun with the two front springs and built the rest round them. Only by carrying out this process in reverse would it be possible to alter the distance between two fixed points which no amount of jacking could effect and between which the spring just would not go. But 'just' is here the operative word, for the job was not an obvious impossibility. On the contrary it was one of those diabolical 'so-near-and-yet-so-far' cases which encourage the unfortunate fitter to go on struggling in the misguided belief that it must simply be a matter of 'wangling' obstinate lumps of metal like the two portions of a Chinese puzzle until precisely the right position is found. In this instance the situation was especially tantalising because we knew that if only we could induce the spring to drop into place, DOLGOCH could be made ready for the road in half an hour. But the time crept remorselessly on to two-fifteen and still the puzzle was no nearer solution. Prospective passengers would be turning up for the afternoon train, so I had to leave David, clean myself up as best I could, open the Wharf office and face the melancholy task of explaining to a succession of disappointed passengers that, as the B.B.C. puts it, there had been a 'technical hitch'. I said it was possible that the train would run but that I would not take any bookings until I received further news from the shed.

One of the difficulties of operating the Talyllyn during this first season, especially with so small a staff, was created by the fact that the office was at one station, and the engineering department at another with no communication between them. This meant that on occasions such as this the luckless individual in charge at the Wharf could only be supplied with news from the shed by breathless emissaries or pedalling furiously between one station and the other when they could have been better employed in helping to overcome the crisis. More often than not I was left at the Wharf in a state of frustrated ignorance to watch the hands of the clock with as much patience as I could muster. At such times I found the role of 'Public Relations Officer' acutely embarrassing. To arrive at the terminal headquarters of a railway company and find a notice to the effect that: 'The 2.45 p.m. train will run approximately 30 minutes late' may be annoying but at least it shows some evidence of organisation. But to be greeted by an official who can only say 'I'm sorry to say we've had a bit of trouble and I can't tell you yet whether we shall be able to run the 2.45' is a contingency scarcely calculated to inspire confidence. On this particular occasion, sad to relate, the 2.45 did not run. David struggled on, the melancholy afternoon wore slowly away, and it was not until the last disappointed would-be passenger had departed that the spring went home at last. This ultimate victory, I may add, was only achieved by the brutal expedient of burning away with an oxy-acetylene torch one of the two fixed points between which the spring positively refused to go. For the information of locomotive men, the parts thus drastically treated were the top corners of what are called the horn cheeks.

If anything was required to convince us of the need to get a second locomotive into service as soon as possible it was these two episodes of the errant eccentric and the shattered spring. Accordingly, in the intervals of ministering to DOLGOCH'S maladies, David was pressing on with his work on No. 3 SIR HAYDN. As well as a considerable amount of detail work which I need not enumerate, it was necessary to strip the boiler of this engine for inspection, a job which involved removing most of the boiler mountings, the saddle tank, the coal bunkers and part of the cab. I should at this point describe in some detail the shops at Pendre, otherwise someone accustomed to a more normal motive power depot may wonder why it was not until late July that No. 3 was ready for steam.

The scene of the labours I have so far described was the running shed which, in theory, was reserved for locomotives in service. In practice, at this time, No. 1 TALYLLYN lay slumbering at the back of it. Here there were no repair facilities whatsoever apart from the pit. There were barrels of oil, a sack of cotton waste and, high up under the roof where it was supported on a framework of old rails, a large wooden water tank which leaked so ominously that it looked as if it might burst at any moment. This threatened inundation was another of those things which haunted me like the story of the runaway wagons at the Wharf, for the old tank was our sole source of locomotive water supply at Towyn. It had originally been filled by a typical Talyllyn contrivance consisting of a steam water lifter sunk in a well just outside the shed which used to be coupled up to the boiler of whichever engine happened to be in steam. Happily for us, however, the tank had since been connected to the town supply although even this improvement was not so great as one might suppose. For, apart from the excessive leakage, no one had thought of fitting a ball valve in the tank to cut off the inflow when it was full, and this meant that the supply tap had to be turned on and off as required. As the flow from the mains was very slow, someone must needs remember to turn on the tap long before it was required to fill a locomotive tank, and the price for forgetfulness was an immediate water crisis. There was one indeed fatal occasion of an evening special train when Dai Jones, misled by this departure from the usual daily routine, forgot to turn on the tap. Eventually, after a delay of twenty anxious minutes, the locomotive appeared at the Wharf with (in Dai's estimation) just enough water in the tank to take us to Dolgoch. But when the trian reached Brynglas the reassuring song of the injector suddenly faltered. As it coughed, spluttered and finally blew steam through the waste pipe it became only too patently apparent that Dai had woefully miscalculated. There was nothing for it but to borrow buckets from Brynglas farm and replenish the tank from the neighbouring stream. Now on an occasion such as this when the train came to a sudden stop and the passengers observed the driver, the fireman and the guard sprinting off up the hillside, it became impossible to sustain the illusion that this was merely part of the routine of normal working. On the contrary the passengers might have been pardoned for concluding that the boiler was about to explode and that it had become a case of every man for himself. Such were the embarrassing situations which the Pendre water tank could create.

From the back of the running shed there was a small communicating door leading into the Repair Shop, the two buildings being parallel with one another and the main access to the latter being via a line of rails running round the back of the long carriage shed. This road, the southernmost of the five parallel tracks in Pendre yard, ran on to an engine pit similar to the one in the Running Shed. Beside it stood a small fitter's bench with a single vice. At the time we took over, the rest of the equipment consisted of the following: a smith's anvil and forge, the latter blown by a very asthmatic and short-winded pair of bellows; a carpenter's bench littered with empty paint pots and boxes of rusty nails; an old grindstone which had worn decidedly egg-shaped, standing beside a home-made circular saw bench without a saw; hand-operated drill and screwing machines, the latter the most useful item in the shop; a lathe whose bed consisted of two lengths of rail turned upside down. This last item was the only power operated tool surviving in the shop, although the Hornsby horizontal oil engine (*circa* 1910 and incomplete) in the far corner of the shop was connected by belt to quite an impressive length of line shafting. Before the installation of this engine, we were told, the lathe was powered when required by an old blind man who stood on a platform overhead and turned a driving wheel. I cannot vouch for the truth of this latter-day version of the treadmill, but there were certainly brackets on the roof beams which had obviously supported such a platform.

Small equipment consisted mainly of spanners with broken or filed-out jaws and some curious home-made tools of crude form and unknown function which we guessed must have been knocked up in the course of past battles of wits with TALYLLYN or DOLGOCH. There was also a set of stocks and dies of so archaic a pattern that none of us had ever seen their like before. We felt that they ought to be donated to some industrial museum; certainly no amount of ingenuity could induce them to cut a thread. But the striking thing about the Repair Shop was not its equipment, or the lack of it, but the prodigious accumulation of unconsidered trifles or, to put it more crudely, junk. Here, in cupboards, pigeon holes and boxes, on floors, on window-sills or hanging from the walls, was the history of the Talyllyn Railway expressed, not in paper as in the Wharf office, but in terms of cast and wrought iron, steel, brass and wood. Here were old Giffard injectors, broken steam gauges, steam valves with stripped threads, wooden patterns and the grisly relics of many a bygone disaster in the form of tired or broken springs, mangled bolts and seized or cracked bearing brasses. And all were covered in a thick layer of dust thanks to old Peter's chickens which scratched and ruffled undisturbed on the earth floor. This, then, was the Swindon of the Talyllyn where our locomotive work had to be done.

Apart from a couple of useful jacks, our only lifting apparatus was a rusty block and tackle attached by a chain to one of the roof trusses. When the moment came to use this device to lift the saddle tank off No. 3, David and I contemplated the prospect with some misgiving. The roof beam looked so rotten where it went into the damp wall from which ferns were growing, that we were afraid that instead of lifting the tank to the roof we might very well succeed in pulling the roof down to the tank. But we evidently under-estimated the roof's powers of resistance, for while we were debating the question we were joined by old Mr Hugh Jones (not Dai's father, but another ex-employee of the railway of long standing). This worthy laughed heartily at our misgivings and pointed to an odd length of line shafting which lay across our beam and its neighbour. It was of solid steel about two and a half inches in diameter, and somehow or other it had acquired a very pronounced bend in the middle. That bend, the old man alleged, had been achieved when they were removing the boiler from TALYLLYN during the reframing job and had discovered that, as a result of some oversight, they were trying to lift the complete locomotive. After this reassuring piece of information we very soon had the saddle tank off and safely lowered to the ground.

When the boiler had been completely stripped we received another visit from our friend the boiler inspector. The weakness of the boiler, as we realised, was the state of the tubes, but out of consideration for our difficulties the inspector agreed to pass the boiler for service at reduced pressure upon the understanding that it would be retubed before it put in another year's work. The task of reassembly and of getting the engine ready for steam then began, and in this we received invaluable skilled assistance from two members who were on the staff of the locomotive department of the Eastern Region of British Railways: Bill Harvey, shed-master from Norwich, and his friend Allan Garraway from Liverpool Street.

I have already stressed to how great an extent the success of our railway adventure was dependent on the help of volunteer members of the Society. Indeed the whole scheme was founded on the belief that all lovers of railways would welcome such a unique opportunity to give their interest practical expression by helping to operate and maintain a public railway of such historic interest. In the course of this first season and the next, we certainly did succeed in building up a devoted band of amateur enthusiasts who were eager and willing to tackle any job that came their way from unloading coal wagons to cleaning down locomotives or slaving on the permanent way in gruelling heat or soaking rain. They came again and again, sacrificing not only their annual holidays but their week-ends as well, so that we soon came to look upon them as personal friends and as members of the staff. But it had never occurred to me for a moment that we would also win so much support from professional railwaymen whose long and hard

'Connected by a belt to a quite impressive length of line shafting'. The repair shop much as it was though improvements like electric light have arrived

John Snell

'A week of perfect summer weather helping David in the repair shop'. David with his Lea Francis astride the rails at Pendre

John Snell

The workhorse to get the general manager to the scene. The 1924 Alvis at Pendre

Left: No. 3 is off again, 'an all too common happening' (*Rolt Archive*). Right: 'Consideration and good humour'. Passengers mostly remained calm when difficulties became manifest. A group of the Vintage Sports Car Club: Kent Karslake, Bill Faulkner (driver), Lawrence Pomeroy, Forest Lycett, Tom Rolt, Sam Clutton and Terry Breen deal with a tree (*Rolt Archive*)

experience of the job from the inside left no room for any romantic illusions as to what it takes to keep a railway running. They of all people, I thought, would, if they visited the Talyllyn at all, be most likely to sit back and leave it to others to do the work for a change. Yet Bill Harvey spent a week of perfect summer weather helping David in the repair shop and at the end of it told me he had spent one of the most enjoyable holidays of his life. Nor were he and Allan Garraway the only ones. I can think of at least four other railwaymen, a locomotive fitter, a goods clerk, a draughtsman, and a top-link driver who devoted their holidays to the Talyllyn during this first season, while the next season saw others. In days when so many are only concerned about the size of the pay packet at the end of the week, such men were a splendid tribute to the railway tradition of pride in the job.

With this unexpected professional aid, locomotive No. 3 was made ready for the road and steam was raised in her for the first time on the evening of Friday, July 20th. It was a tense and exciting moment when, with David at the regulator and en- veloped in a hissing cloud of steam from open cylinder drain- cocks, SIR HAYDN backed slowly out of the repair shop into the twilight of that summer's evening. It was also a historic occasion. For the first time in over eighty years a new locomotive was running under its own steam over Talyllyn metals. It was too late to go far afield, but we ran her slowly and cautiously up the line to a point near Fach Goch and then back again through Pendre and down to the Wharf. SIR HAYDN is mounted entirely on coil springs, those over the driving and coupled axles being set in clusters, and after the lumbering, elephantine gait of DOLGOCH she seemed to ride our rough road as lightly and easily as a coach. And after the frenzied winding on of the hand brake which was the only, and not particularly effective way of arresting the 'old lady's' impetuous progress, what a revelation to pull down with finger and thumb the handle of the vacuum ejector and feel the engine come to rest in instant obedience and with no more fuss than the faint sigh of admitted air! When we brought her back to the shed we decided that, the next day being a Saturday, we would give No. 3 a trial run to Abergynolwyn and back.

The morrow turned out to be the warmest day of the year; everything shimmered under a cloudless, brazen sky and metal surfaces became too hot to touch. So it was a sweaty and grimy crew that brought SIR HAYDN into the platform at Pendre immediately after lunch, coupled up to the first class coach and the brake-van. The whistle sounded an unfamiliar note and off we went. As we forged up Hen-dy and Cynfal banks it was exciting to hear for the first time a strange voice at the head of the train, a deep but slightly irregular beat reminiscent of a Midland Compound working hard. Everything went well until we were midway between Rhydyronen and Brynglas. Then the locomotive gave a sudden sickening lurch and reeled along for a yard or two in a cloud of dust before coming to a stand with a jerk. She was off the road. Investigation quickly showed that the track was wide to gauge at this point and that the driving wheels had simply dropped in between the rails. It was our first lesson in the fatal effect of narrower wheel tyres on a road not distinguished for accuracy of gauge. Fortunately we had come prepared with plenty of tools. By dint of much jacking, packing and manoeuvring we got the locomotive back on to the rails, pulled the offending length of track in to gauge and continued on our way. After this incident we proceeded very cautiously indeed but there was no further mishap. We stopped to take on water at Dolgoch and then went on to Abergynolwyn. Confidence was by this time somewhat restored, and on an uneventful return journey we had no difficulty in keeping to time-table schedule. This successful down run gave us grounds for hoping that our derailment had no ominous significance but was simply a piece of bad luck which might never be repeated. We decided to put No. 3 into service as soon as possible, and David and I spent the rest of the week-end covering her dingy red-brown Corris livery in a smart fresh coat of Talyllyn green.

On the morning of the following Tuesday DOLGOCH worked the morning service as usual, but in the afternoon it was SIR HAYDN with David in charge which backed on to the four-coach train at the Wharf. A lighter engine than DOLGOCH, and with part of her weight carried on trailing wheels, it is surprising that No. 3

should have worked for so many years on the difficult Corris road with no proper sanding gear. Although the rail was dry on this afternoon, with the full load of four coaches, she began to slip badly as she approached Ty Mawr bridge until, despite David's delicate handling of a very sensitive regulator, she came to a stand and then started to slide back down the grade. After we had judiciously sanded the rail with the watering can from the van, David succeeded not only in getting her away but in keeping her moving thereafter. But this performance on a dry rail did not augur well for what might happen on a greasy day. Apart from this incident the journey up and down was uneventful, but the passengers on that train little knew that the crew were on tenterhooks and keeping their fingers crossed every yard of the way. And not without cause, for this proved to be the only trouble free turn that SIR HAYDN has so far worked.

It was decided to run No. 3 again the next morning, this time with Dai Jones driving under David's tuition. Instead of firing, John Snell took a turn as guard on this train, thus leaving me free to deal with some overdue correspondence in the Wharf station office. As the hands of the clock approached 12.45 it became more and more difficult to concentrate. I began to strain my ears for the sound of a distant whistle and to glance with increasing frequency and anxiety up the line. 12.50, 12.55, one o'clock came and still there was no sound or sight of the train. Then there came a sudden knock on the door and Mr Parry appeared looking rather hot and breathless. Someone had just telephoned him from the public call box at Abergynolwyn with the message that No. 3 had twice become derailed on the loop points at the terminus and that they were still trying to get her back on the road. What to do now? My first thought was that DOLGOCH must be put into steam at once, so I jumped into my car and drove up to Pendre. My arrival there coincided with that of John Snell who, with the same thought in mind, had managed to get a lift back. Leaving John to light up the engine, I ran back to my car and tore up the winding valley road to Abergynolwyn. As I drove I considered what would be the best plan of action. There appeared to be two alternatives. The train had been a light one, and two coaches, 'Limping Lulu' and the other 'Third', had been left behind at the Wharf. I had instructed John, as soon as he got steam on DOLGOCH, to back down on to these two coaches and then to await further developments. With the season nearing its peak the afternoon service was running very full so it was quite obvious that we could not hope to pack all the passengers into two coaches. But if the worst came to the worst, with these and the Corris brake-van we could at least maintain the service however inadequately, and could then make up the complete train at Abergynolwyn, leaving No. 3 to follow us down light as best she could. The alternative was the hope that we could get SIR HAYDN re-railed and back to the Wharf in time to allow the 2.45 to get away without too much delay.

I arrived at Abergynolwyn to find that No. 3 had run well and truly amok on the points at the top end of the loop. David, Dai, Bill Oliver and two or three volunteers were working feverishly with jacks, packing, crowbars and odd lengths of rail to get her back on the road while the stranded passengers, happily not too numerous, sat disconsolately on the grass thinking of their lost lunch. Unfortunately at this time we possessed no re-railing ramps in our equipment, and the job was proving extremely awkward. I stayed to help for as long as I dared and finally, at twenty past two, just as I had realised that I must return, I had the belated satisfaction of seeing No. 3 back on the road at last. I decided to take the risk that she would get her train back to Towyn without another derailment, and, after asking David to start the train as soon as possible, I rushed back to the Wharf to find a puzzled crowd assembled by the locked door of the booking-office. Trying to assume an air of bland official confidence which I certainly did not feel, I explained that the 2.45 train would leave late because it must await the arrival of a down train which had been delayed up the line. I knew that David would not be so foolhardy as to try to make up lost time with No. 3, so I estimated that 3.30 would be zero hour for her arrival. Meanwhile the arrival of DOLGOCH encouraged the patiently waiting passengers. She coupled up to the two coaches on the siding which were already full and stood there gently simmering. As the time moved round to the half-hour I found myself in a state of considerable suspense for the second time that day. Was the gamble going to come off? Would it have been wiser after all to run that second train of two coaches? For if No. 3 misbehaved again on the way back we might not be able to run an afternoon train at all, and then all these passengers would be disappointed. I had just come to the conclusion that I had made a fatal error of judgment when from the direction of the cutting I heard the blessed sound of a locomotive whistle. In a few moments more, and on the stroke of 3.30, No. 3 ran under the bridge. As she rolled into the station and brought her train to a stop with a final sigh from the vacuum brake, she made so brave a sight in her fresh green livery and seemed to bring with her such an assured air of efficiency that the waiting passengers, little knowing what had been going on up the line, must have wondered what could have caused the delay.

That was a memorable day in the history of the Wharf station. In the first place there was the unprecedented spectacle of two engines in steam, and in the second it witnessed what I am sure must have been the quickest turn round of trains ever performed on the Talyllyn. For as soon as the train came to a standstill, DOLGOCH pulled her two coaches out of the siding and backed on. Exactly four minutes after No. 3's arrival 'the old lady' pulled out with a full train of four coaches. She was just over three-quarters of an hour behind time, but we had lost no revenue and I had heard no grumbles from the passengers. It was only afterwards that I learnt from David how close a call it had been. For SIR HAYDN's trailing wheels had jumped the road as they were running into Pendre, but had fortunately re-railed themselves.

This behaviour of No. 3, which was really the fault of our permanent way, was a major tragedy and a bitter blow to our hopes. We had been relying upon this little locomotive, in many ways the most handsome engine in our stud, to relieve DOLGOCH of the heaviest burden of traffic, and an immense amount of hard work had been put in to this end. But now, although the peak holiday season was upon us, I felt that it was not safe to run her in view of what had happened. I was influenced in this decision by the fact that at this time David had to leave us for a fortnight to attend to urgent business of his own. I decided that it would be best to concentrate upon keeping DOLGOCH running while he was away and that we would only consider giving SIR HAYDN another trial after he had returned.

It was obvious that we would need all the passenger accommodation we could muster during August Bank Holiday week, so I decided that the little Corris brake-van must be furbished up without delay. It was still in its original drab grey livery having been used so far only as a 'permanent way brake', a useful repository where tools could be kept under lock and key. This decision to prepare the Corris van for passenger use proved a very timely one, for on almost every day of August it was required for the afternoon service, and even with this extra accommodation many potential passengers had to be turned away. I had felt very doubtful about the ability of DOLGOCH to withstand for very long such a weight of traffic without some major catastrophe. But any harsh and unprintable names I may have called her in moments of stress in the shed were now forgotten and forgiven in my admiration for this ancient locomotive as day after day she toiled bravely up the long gradients with a train of four coaches and two vans packed with a load of as many as a hundred and twenty passengers. During the first fortnight of August when the heaviest traffic of the whole season was carried, the only delays which could be laid at the door of the motive power department were due to occasional bad steaming. I have already said that DOLGOCH was a tricky steamer, and with a heavy train the smallest human error in firing or the slightest defect could seriously reduce her steaming capacity. One of the most frequent sources of trouble was that, owing to the battering she received on the rough road, air leaks would develop in the smoke-box round the base of the blast pipe. Naturally, this partially destroyed the vacuum created in the smoke-box by the blast and consequently reduced its 'pull' on the fire. Stopping these leaks with fire cement became a regular shed chore, but even so the cement would sometimes break up on the road and then at once the trouble would start. I could always tell from the brake-van whether or not all was well with 'the old lady' by the sound of her whistle. Her

'He must cling with one hand while with the other he dribbles sand down the pipe of the engine's only sand-box.' Gareth Jones engaged in a more primitive mode from the buffer team of No. 4

Graham Vincent

'Credit for this achievement was due, I felt, to one gallant old locomotive.' DOLGOCH on works train at Rhydyronen

John Snell

'More relaying had been done'. A new loop and relaying at Abergynolwyn

John Snell

normal, healthy voice was a piercing scream, urgent and self-important as though to say 'Look out everybody, here I come.' So if I heard instead only a faint and plaintive note with a dying fall like the opening music in *Twelfth Night*, then I knew very well that the engine crew were trying desperately to jockey her along to the next station with a mere twenty-five pounds 'on the clock' and the water level hovering near the bottom fitting of the gauge glass. However badly she was steaming we always did our utmost to uphold prestige by running non-stop from station to station and then prolonging station stops in order to 'blow up'. In this we were usually, though not invariably, successful. Such protracted station stops might make the passenger impatient but if, as was commonly the case at this season, he knew little or nothing of the mysteries of steam locomotives or of railway working in general, he could be kept in ignorance of the cause of the delay and deluded into believing that the situation, however aggravating, was under control. But if the train came to an ignominious and breathless halt in mid-section no amount of dissimulation could conceal from the most ignorant passenger that all was not well.

The only serious delay to a train which occurred during the first part of August was occasioned by the activities of our permanent way department and was due to one of those unpredictable happenings which can play havoc with the best laid plans. It was a day of great heat, and the gang were carrying out some repairs to the line between Pendre and Ty Mawr bridge which included changing a defective rail. The new rail lay beside the track ready to go in, and after the down morning train had passed the old rail was lifted out. In the ordinary way there would have been ample time to complete the job before the 2.45 was due to pass, but when the new rail was manoeuvred into place they found to their consternation that it was nearly an inch too long. This was not due to any miscalculation. Both rails were, in fact, the same length. What had happened was that as soon as the old rail had been removed, rail expansion due to the extreme heat had closed the gap by that amount. By no effort could the gap be widened, and finally Bill and his mates were reduced to sawing the crucial inch off the end of the rail by hand while the crowded train waited impatiently in the platform at Pendre. We were forty-five minutes behind time when we at last received an 'all clear' hand signal from the curve.

David's very welcome return to Towyn coincided with a staff crisis. He and John Snell turned up at the shed one morning to find that although DOLGOCH had been lit up there was no sign of her driver. Dai Jones had let us down as badly as his father had done just before Whitsun by walking out without notice. Happily this emergency was soon satisfactorily overcome. John Snell was promoted to driver, a duty he has continued to perform with great success, while his place as fireman was filled, during school holidays, by Gareth Jones, a local boy who, despite his youth, turned out to be an excellent fireman and a born railwayman. Prior to this, too, the staff position had already been eased by the addition of one of our most helpful volunteers, A.D. Maguire, who agreed to team up with Bill Oliver on the permanent way until the end of the season. An Irishman and an ex-member of the Indian Police Force, Maguire was a stolid, imperturbable man, inclined to be taciturn but with a wry and occasionally cynical sense of humour. As Bill Oliver was tall and thin with a mercurial temperament and a ceaseless flow of talk there could scarcely have been a greater contrast between the two men. Perhaps it was because one was such a foil to the other that they worked so well together. In the event, 'Maggie', as he was invariably called, continued to work on the railway until the end of the year, when he went overseas, and during that time the sight of his stocky figure was always reassuring on any occasion of trouble.

With this reconstituted staff things proceeded smoothly enough until I decided to give SIR HAYDN another trial. She was rostered for the morning train on the seventeenth of August, a day doomed to be the blackest of the season. On the up journey all went well, but on the return SIR HAYDN's trailing wheels became derailed and then re-railed themselves between Abergynolwyn and Dolgoch. In the woods below Dolgoch they left the road again and this time, not only did they fail to re-rail themselves but, by spreading the rails, they succeeded in derailing one of the following coaches. This was the first derailment of the passenger stock which we had experienced. Fortunately we had been travelling very slowly at the time and, as they clambered out, the occupants of the coach did not betray any symptoms of undue alarm. We managed to get the coach and the pony truck of the locomotive back on to the road only to discover that another of the coaches was quite immovable. By some extraordinary mischance a large lump of wood (it looked like part of the root of a tree) had become so firmly wedged between the rim of a wheel and the horn bracket that the wheel was locked and no amount of pushing or pulling would free it. It had to be hacked out with hammer and chisel, a proceeding which took longer than the rerailing, and we arrived back at Towyn an hour behind time. In view of this incident I decided that we must abandon the luckless experiment and run DOLGOCH that afternoon, but even so the troubles of that day were not over.

We were running down from Abergynolwyn with a full train and I was talking to a newly arrived volunteer who was travelling with me in the van. He had just asked me whether we had many derailments, and I had replied with a confident 'No' when the van gave a sudden lurch and proceeded to run along the roadbed with a series of shattering jolts and crashing sounds until DOLGOCH could be pulled up. We then found that the Corris van at the tail of the train was also off the road and at the very same point where No. 3 had first become derailed that morning. It was evident that, as on the second occasion, she had spread the rails to a dangerous extent and so laid a trap for the next train. Once again we set about the job of re-railing with all possible speed, but for the second time that day we arrived back at Towyn an hour late.

At this point I may anticipate a little by relating the last sad paragraph in the history of SIR HAYDN down to the time of writing. It had become painfully obvious that, as she stood, the locomotive was not safe for public service, but latterly the trouble had been confined to the very small trailing wheels which, by all accounts, had proved troublesome on the Corris line. So I decided to make the final experiment of increasing the tread width by turning down part of the treads and shrinking on extensions. The wheels were removed and sent away to a member with an engineering business in the Black Country. He dealt with them with most commendable speed and efficiency and returned them to us looking more like rollers than wheels. When they had been refitted, No. 3 was given a last chance; not, this time, on a service train but on a special ballast train one Saturday afternoon. She travelled well enough as far as Dolgoch, but on the last section to Abergynolwyn her driving wheels suddenly dropped between the rails just as they had done on the occasion of her first trial. So SIR HAYDN stands to-day sadly cold and lifeless in the shed at Pendre. For the edification of members and visitors the little locomotive is kept as clean and smart as ever, but there she is likely to remain until either considerable improvements have been made to the permanent way, or her driving wheels can be re-tyred.

Meanwhile all our hopes of maintaining the service until the end of September now rested in DOLGOCH, but that her recent spell of exemplary behaviour would last much longer was altogether too much to expect. Sure enough, only three days after the black seventeenth of August the next serious mishap occurred. The afternoon train was standing well filled at the Wharf and I was awaiting the appearance of the engine from the shed. Imagine then my consternation when I saw coming down the cutting, not the welcome rear view of DOLGOCH, but the engine crew hurrying along the line on foot. They had been steaming through the cutting as usual on their way to the Wharf when the jolt of a more than usually rough rail joint had dislodged the fire bar ring. As a result the whole fire, bars and all, had been disgorged on to the track in a flaming heap. As if this was not enough, in its fall the fire bar ring had struck one of the expansion links, damaging the ring and bending one of the eccentric rods. Faced with such a catalogue of misfortune we might have been forgiven for cancelling the train, but it was tacitly accepted amongst us that if it was humanly possible the train should run. So the crippled locomotive limped back to the shed on the steam that remained in the boiler, the damaged ring and rod were straightened and refitted, the bars put back, the fire relit and an hour and a half later the belated train pulled out. True, some of the passengers had grown tired of waiting, but we still carried a fair complement.

'No. 3 was given her last chance' (she failed it, for the moment)

Left: No. 3 is re-railed, again. Right: 'Investigation quickly showed that the track was wide to gauge at this point'.
Troubles with No. 3 as described in Chapter Four

(John Snell)

Pendre workshop old form. No. 3 as stripped by David Curwen in 1951

John Adams

'If No. 4 fulfilled expectations, these would be two serviceable locomotives available'. She did, after her boiler was renewed through the good offices of John Alcock of Hunslet of Leeds (they had built her). Picture shows 1952 inaugural double-headed train. No. 4, EDWARD THOMAS's tank is flat workshop grey and Bill Oliver drives No. 2

J.C. Flemons

The ways of locomotives, particularly of veterans like DOL-GOCH, are unpredictable. On this occasion we had succeeded in maintaining the service in spite of a most dire and spectacular calamity, yet a week later the morning train had to be cancelled for a reason of the most maddening triviality. David was feeling unwell that morning and had not come down to the shed, so that when a breathless Gareth Jones appeared at the Wharf to say that DOLGOCH's injector would not work there was nothing to be done but to lock the office and go back with him to Pendre. It was at once obvious that the feed pipe between the tank and the injector was choked, but it was nearly departure time so to avoid delay I advised the crew to work on the other, offside injector. This was normally held in reserve in case of emergency and was regarded as suspect because of the condition of the clack valve on this side of the boiler. But when we tried it, it worked immediately and perfectly, singing a most reassuring song, so I set off back to the Wharf, leaving the crew to bring the engine down. Ten minutes later I was just about to give the 'right away' when, with a sudden roar, DOLGOCH almost vanished from sight in a cloud of escaping steam. John had put his injector on and the clack had stuck open. Agitated heads popped out of carriage windows as I ran forward, my first thought being to shut off the clack. Unfortunately on the type of valve with which 'the old lady' is fitted there is no means of isolating the clack valve from the boiler, the manual control operating simply by holding this valve down on to its seating. Hence it was quite useless in this event of something becoming lodged under the valve. After a few seconds desperate tapping with a hammer on the body of the valve in the vain hope of clearing it, it became quite obvious that the only thing to be done was to run back to shed with all speed while there was still some water in the boiler and there to drop the fire. DOLGOCH was hurriedly uncoupled and in a moment the abandoned passengers saw with dismay the engine of their train, still roaring and belching steam, disappearing up the line as fast as she could go. I was then left with the unhappy task of explaining that there could be no train that morning. For the clack valve could not be touched until steam was off, and by the time the boiler had been filled again, the fire relit and steam raised, it would be far too late. All that had caused this ignominious locomotive failure was a piece of hard scale, little larger than a grain of corn, which had become firmly wedged on the seating of the clack valve. As for the other injector, a small lump of cotton waste which had been accidently dropped into the tank at some time or other had found its way into the feed pipe.

This incident occurred at the end of August when the English holiday invasion had almost spent its force and was beginning to ebb away. Throughout the next and last month of the season the burden on our sorely tried old locomotive became progressively lighter. Indeed there was only one more serious operational hitch and that was not due to any fit of temperament on the part of 'the old lady' but was the bitter fruit of an unsuccessful experiment. As such it dealt a damaging blow to our prestige besides landing us in a predicament of peculiar difficulty. It all began when a newly arrived volunteer expressed concern at the amount of slack coal we were wasting. We had always acted on the assumption that DOLGOCH, at the best of times an uncertain steamer, would not effectively burn slack in so small a firebox, and so there was a sizeable heap of sieved-out slack outside Pendre shed. But our volunteer, who was a man of considerable experience, insisted that it was simply a question of firing technique, so we decided to give him an opportunity to prove his words on the afternoon train. The consequences could scarcely have been more disastrous.

I did not accompany the train on this particular occasion and so did not know that anything was amiss until shortly before it was due in when I saw, with dire foreboding, some passengers walking back down the line. Fortunately, being so late in the season, they were not too numerous and, as I afterwards discovered, those who had not walked were ferried back by road by the permanent way gang. The train, they said, had failed for lack of steam near Brynglas on the up journey. Sure enough I found DOLGOCH standing about a quarter of a mile short of Brynglas with a dead fire, no water showing in the gauge glass and only a drop left in the tank. I had always dreaded some catastrophe which would involve having to leave DOLGOCH and her train stranded somewhere on the line overnight. So far, no matter what tribulations the day had brought we had always managed to sleep sound in the knowledge that the train was safely housed at Pendre and ready for the next morning's work. But now, if the situation was to be saved we should have to work hard and quickly, for these September evenings no longer gave us so handsome a margin of daylight. So David and I, assisted by Bill Oliver, set to work. First of all we cleared the grate, removing enough unburnt slack coal from the firebox to fill a wheelbarrow. Next we unscrewed the boiler filling plug and with the aid of a bucket and a funnel borrowed from a neighbouring farm, managed to transfer, via the injector waste pipe, enough water from the near empty tank to the boiler to bring the level back into the bottom of the gauge glass. We then replaced the plug, lit up the fire and awaited events. As the boiler was still hot she did not take too long to steam and we then drew the train up to Brynglas station where, for the second time in the season, we proceeded to fill up the tank with buckets from the stream. By the time this had been accomplished it was nine o'clock and the autumn dusk had deepened into a night in which there was as yet no moon. We held a short conference on the station platform and decided not to run the train back to Towyn with all the difficulties which this entailed, but to leave the coaches on the Brynglas siding and run the engine up to Dolgoch to stand by the water column there overnight. David and I were both living at Dolgoch so it would be a simple matter to light her up again in the morning, fill up her tank and then run back to Towyn in time to work the morning service, picking up the train at Brynglas en route. As both David and I had our cars at Brynglas it was arranged that he should drive the locomotive up to Dolgoch alone while I went there by road so that I could ferry him back again to Brynglas to collect his car.

Of all the crowded recollections of this first season, the one which stays with me most clearly is of my wait on the silent and deserted platform at Dolgoch that night for David to arrive. I must have either under-estimated my own speed or over-estimated his, for I remember wondering uneasily whether some fresh disaster had overtaken him in the darkness. I stood on the platform for some time straining my ears but could hear nothing but the plash of water falling from the overflow of the column. Then I walked through the rock cutting, a pitch black cavern under the overhanging trees, to the end of the viaduct. Through a trellis work of branches I could see that the moon was rising, a harvest moon nearing the full, for although it was not yet visible a waxing, golden light threw into sharp silhouette the massive, rounded shoulder of mountain that brooded over Dolgoch. The night was very still and silent. Only from the darkness of the ravine below the viaduct there sounded the murmur of the stream, the more distant thunder of the falls and, occasionally, the quavering cry of owls calling to one another from slope to wooded slope. At last there could be heard, very faintly at first and intruding upon the night's serenity with most bizarre effect, that unmistakable clanking and clattering sound which heralded the approach of 'the old lady'. In a few moments I could see at the end of the long tunnel of trees beyond the viaduct the single yellow eye of her headlight growing gradually larger and flickering and swaying like a will-o'-the-wisp as she rolled and jolted along the track. When she rumbled over the viaduct I flashed my torch and she came to a stop in the cutting. She stood there under the trees like some ancient dragon, hissing gently to herself, the glare from her grate casting a fiery rectangle of light between the rails. 'Where am I?' called a voice from the darkness of her cab; 'have I been over the viaduct yet?' Together we took DOLGOCH on to the water column and bedded her down for her night out. The rest was easy. Another, and, as it proved, the last, hazard of the season had been successfully overcome.

Had it not been for these vicissitudes this book would not, as I have said, justify its title, but I do not want this account of them to create any distorted impression of the reliability of the Talyllyn Railway. For it is by no means only on the Talyllyn that such troubles can occur. Even on the best regulated railways more defects develop on the road than the travelling public ever realises. When their train pulls into the terminus a few minutes behind time the passengers grumble, little knowing that, through no fault of their own, the driver had been using all the mastery of his craft to nurse a sick locomotive home or that his fireman has been waging a desperate fight for steam. The story of these struggles never reaches the public whereas I have taken you behind the scenes.

Time and again, as the weeks went by, our service was maintained with exemplary punctuality. Any delay of fifteen minutes or more was exceptional, and was usually due to no fault of ours. The most frequent cause of late running was the unpunctuality of our nationalised neighbours at Towyn, especially that of the train due in from Barmouth at 2.37 with which our 2.45 was scheduled to connect. This Coast line, in common with the greater part of the old Cambrian system is, of course, single and the real offender in this instance was the train in the opposite direction which the 2.37 was booked to cross at Llwyngwril. This train, due at Towyn at 2 p.m., carried connections from Shrewsbury and Birmingham Snow Hill as well as from Crewe and Manchester and was often very late, particularly during the holiday season. Thus our train would wait impatiently at the terminus while a member of the crew stood on the edge of the Wharf and looked down the line for a sign of the errant connection until: 'She's signalled,' he would call, or 'She's running into the platform now.' On these occasions, when DOLGOCH pulled into Abergynolwyn a quarter of an hour late, it was strange to reflect that the cause of the delay, if traced back, might prove to be bad station work in Manchester, a trifling error on the part of Train Control at Crewe or the consequences of a 'hot box' in Birmingham. Yet in the intricate organisation of our railway system such is the far-flung repercussion of the most minor fault. Needless to say, this chain of events did not operate in reverse. No main line connections waited for us, so that no 'new liner' with through coaches from mid-Wales arrived late at Paddington because our 'old lady' had had a fit of the sulks and refused to steam.

Was it boring to travel up and down the valley twice daily as I did throughout most of this first season? I did not find it so. No two journeys were the same and none lacked incident if only of a minor kind. There were, for example, the continual diversions caused by straying livestock. Barring only escapes from a circus it is difficult to think of many creatures wild or domesticated which

113

did not at some time or another frequent the Talyllyn track. I have seen weasels, stoats, red squirrels (for their enemy the grey squirrel has not yet invaded this part of Wales), rabbits, hares and, on one occasion, a fox, but they were all much too shy to risk an encounter with DOLGOCH at close quarters. But in all domestic creatures, even sheep dogs, the sight of DOLGOCH seemed to inspire the most marked suicidal tendencies. Whereas in similar circumstances they would move out of the path of a faster moving car and allow it to pass, the ponderous approach of 'the old lady' appeared to reduce them to a state at once hypnotised and panic-stricken. They refused to turn aside from the line ahead, so that we were forced to adapt the speed of the train to suit the varying gait of straying horses, cows, bullocks, sheep, chickens, ducks, geese and, on one particularly trying occasion, a sow with a litter of small piglets. After a time a gradual slackening of the pace would seem to indicate exhaustion and inspire sympathy for the pursued. But if the fireman (as frequently happened) jumped from the cab to launch a surprise outflanking movement, any humanitarian feelings were speedily quenched. For invariably his quarry responded with a turn of speed that would have eluded a champion sprinter. By far the most numerous and tiresome of these trespassers on the Talyllyn were the sheep. No matter whether we went faster or slower, no matter how we whistled, blew steam, uttered wild cries or waved our arms, or how broad and obvious were the means of escape lying open on either hand, nothing would deflect these sheep from the 'two foot' a yard or so in front of DOLGOCH's buffer beam. Finally, one more than usually suicidal ewe came to an untimely end on the 'Corris Straight', and as a result of this gory and regrettable episode our driver has ever since been known as 'Butcher' Snell. Happily this was the only casualty of the season although old Peter's cockerel lost all but one of his fine green plume of tail feathers as a result of a near miss in Pendre Yard.

The constantly changing complement of the train was another factor which precluded any sense of monotony. Admittedly this involved answering the same questions over and over again, and listening to the same facetious jokes at our expense. Yet it is not these that I remember but rather the conversations I had with the many keenly interested people who came from all over Britain to travel with us up the valley. Among those who spent a day with us towards the end of this first season was T.E.B. Clarke, script writer to Ealing Studios, who had heard of our activities and thought they might make a suitable subject for a film. As a result, some of the episodes I have recorded here, notably the occasion of the water crisis at Brynglas, were incorporated with appropriate artistic and comic licence, in the film 'The Titfield Thunderbolt'. At the time I hoped that our 'old lady' might be cast for the name part, but that was not to be.

Apart from any railway incidents there were always the changes of weather and season in the valley which made no two journeys alike. For how responsive was this mountain landscape to the swift changes of a seaboard climate; one hour dead, oppressive and sombre under leaden skies and the next alight and alive under sunlight and the sweeping shadows of full-sailing clouds. On one journey the sea might be scarcely visible, yet on the next I would be able to see from the van as we ran back to Towyn the shape of Bardsey Island standing far out across the bay. And then I would reflect on the probability that some of Bardsey's many pilgrims may have come by way of the mountain road from Machynlleth to Rhydyronen, which was old long before the present coast road was thought of. If they did so, then surely they would pause when they reached the ridge of Bryn Dinas and for the first time saw before them the object of their quest, the Island of Saints.

Then, too, I had seen from the van the rhythm of the season almost complete its cycle; I had watched hay and corn grow and ripen to harvest, seen the fields briefly patterned by swathe and stook and then grow bare again. I had come with the primroses and had watched the flame of gorse and the mist of bluebells in the woods fade and become forgotten in the splendour of foxglove spires and dog roses in the tangled hedgerows beside the line. But now the plough was out in the fields, the bracken was turning, and these hedgerows were heavy with the fruits of autumn; scarlet of hip and haw and mountain ash, purple of sloe and wild damson, and the dark lustre of blackberries of matchless size.

And so, almost before we realised it, the last day of the season had arrived and many came to speed the last train on its way whom we had not seen since that Whit Monday 'dress rehearsal' which now seemed so long ago. Our experiences since then may have made us wiser men but they certainly had not saddened or discouraged us. Not only had we succeeded in maintaining the service throughout the season, but the Talyllyn Railway had carried the record total of 15,000 passengers. And the biggest share of the credit for this achievement was due, I felt, to one gallant old locomotive.

Chapter Five

During the long, dark winter months DOLGOCH lay slumbering in her shed at Pendre, making only occasional sorties up the valley to fetch a load of ballast from Quarry Siding, and the mountains almost forgot the echo of her shrill whistle. A stranger coming by chance upon the tenuous line of rusting rails might have been forgiven for supposing that the railway had been abandoned, yet this was far from the case. All through the winter the work of improvement went on with the result that when I returned to Towyn in the early spring it was to find that many of the operational hazards of the previous year had either disappeared already or were in process of removal. For example, the Wharf station had been transformed. After eighty-six years it now possessed a platform, a run round loop and, at the end of the platform road, a substantial buffer stop. This put an end to the unorthodox method of reversing the train and to my constant dread that this would eventually result in the coaches crashing off the end of the Wharf. Moreover, the whole section between the Wharf and Pendre had been completely relaid including the main line points at both stations. These last had been assembled from ex-Corris and Welsh Highland Railway material, the components from the latter being almost as good as new thanks to the short working life of that unfortunate railway. No longer would 'the old lady' rock like a ship in distress over worn out points as she ran through Pendre yard.

Another ancient enemy, the old wooden water tank in Pendre Shed, had been given a well-merited and long overdue quietus. Its successor stood outside the shed in such a position that engines could now be watered when standing either on the shed road or in the station platform. This new tank consisted of part of the cooling tank of the old Hornsby oil engine in the Repair Shop mounted upon a substantial stone base. Needless to say, its supply from the mains was now controlled by a ball cock, so that lapse of memory could not longer lead to the embarrassing shortages which had enlivened the previous season.

Both the Running Shed and the Repair Shop had been wired for electric light, so that in any future battles with refractory locomotives we would at least have the advantage of good light instead of being dependent on the smoky flicker of tallow dips. Better still, thanks to the efforts of a volunteer, a private telephone line had been installed between the shed and the Wharf station office. No longer need the hapless individual endeavouring to control the situation at the terminus on occasion of crisis be kept in a state of agonised suspense through ignorance of what was happening in the motive power department.

The Wharf office now also boasted a national telephone. Its installation had been a simple matter of running wires to the building from a neighbouring pole by the roadside, but unlike our own internal line, this had taken months to complete. Although we had secured 'top priority' for this telephone in the spring of the previous year, the only activity during the months that followed had been the periodic appearance of individuals who stood in the Wharf yard gazing earnestly aloft as though scanning the sky for the appearance of hostile aircraft. But any question about telephones produced an effect of shocked surprise and sent them hurrying away. When, in the early autumn, two men arrived and, after indulging in the now familiar sky gazing ritual, did actually proceed to wire the building, I was foolish and ignorant enough to suppose that they would finish the job by installing the instrument. The air of offended dignity with which they informed me that this last was a matter for the fitter and not for them was an appropriate rebuke for my impetuosity and lack of tact. The fact was, of course, that my sojourn on the Talyllyn Railway, where each man must play many parts, had made me forget the new world of the 'closed shop' where it is tantamount to high treason for a carpenter to touch a paint brush or for a painter to drive home a nail. If, I reflected, the staff of our railway was ever compelled to observe this principle of division of labour with such

This evocatively atmospheric shot of No. 4 approaching Pendre. 'A handyman in the fullest and best sense of that term', Pop (Isaac) Davies had, as described, built the new water tower seen left. 'As he worked he assured onlookers that a statue of Sir Haydn Jones was to be placed on top'

Michael Peto

'No longer would "the old lady" rock like a ship in distress over worn out points as she ran through Pendre yard.' A later view, looking up the line at Pendre, from the spectacle plate of No. 6 and showing the relaid track

J.I.C. Boyd

nice distinction, then in our case the 'closed shop' would become no mere figure of speech. The doors of Pendre shed would soon close for good and all. However, the last act of this solemn ritual was ultimately played out and so the Talyllyn Railway received its telephone.

It was not only at the Towyn end of the line that improvements had been made. More relaying had been done at the lower end of the 'Corris Straight' and near Brynglas station, while the top loop at Abergynolwyn had been entirely renewed and lengthened, the station platform being extended to suit. The old loop could only just accommodate a full train of four coaches and two vans, while its condition had been such as to cause considerable concern to waiting passengers.

New equipment was arriving to speed the work of the permanent way department, notably a portable generating set and two electric ballast tamping machines supplied on loan through the good offices of a friend of mine. These machines gave us quite a snob complex, for the local platelayers of British Railways possessed no such modern aids, and for the first time in its history the Talyllyn Railway could fairly claim to be more progressive than its broad gauge neighbour.

Credit for much of the work which had been done during early spring was due to Bill Oliver's father-in-law, Isaac Davies, who had joined the regular staff following 'Maggie's' departure overseas. 'Pop', as he was invariably called, soon proved himself an immense asset to the railway, for he was a handy man in the fullest and best sense of the term. In appearance he reminded me of a benevolent gnome, a small, slight man, quick and deft in movement with rounded shoulders, a pronounced cast in one eye and an infectious grin. He was, among other things, a skilled stone mason and in any difficulty he was a master of ingenious expedient. If a wall threatened to fall or a roof to collapse, if a pipe should burst, a ditch become choked or a locomotive run off the rails the remedy was always to 'ask Pop'. And the little man was never at a loss. Illustrating his speech with a wealth of graphic gesture, pulling imaginary ropes or throwing his weight on to hypothetical levers, he would at once explain how, in his opinion,

119

the job should be tackled, interjecting an occasional interrogative 'D'ye see?' To this the only possible answer was an affirmative and sometimes dishonest nod, for it was not only impossible to interrupt the rapid flow of his speech, but he spoke so softly and sibilantly and with so strong a Welsh intonation that it was not easy to hear exactly what he was saying. But whatever it was, it almost invariably turned out to be correct.

It was 'Pop' who, in an astonishingly short time, erected the substantial stone pillar which supported the new water tank at Pendre. It was a joy to watch this local man handling his native stone with the craftsman's assured and instinctive mastery of his material. The spirits of the men who had built the great dry walls which march over the Merioneth mountains surely guided the hands that unerringly selected the right stone from the pile beside him, or with a precise tap of a hammer found the grain and trimmed an awkward block to his purpose. And as he worked he assured inquisitive onlookers that a statue of Sir Haydn Jones was to be placed on the top of his column.

Not only on the permanent way but in the motive power department there had been progress made, although the evidence of this was not yet visible at Towyn. After the fiasco of SIR HAYDN the previous season, David had turned his attention to the second Corris locomotive, No. 4, EDWARD THOMAS, and it soon became clear that the boiler of this engine required far more extensive repair than we had supposed. The work would be very difficult, if not impossible, to carry out efficiently in our primitive Repair Shop, yet the need for a reliable second locomotive was vital. At this juncture, by a most fortuitous piece of good fortune, Mr John Alcock, the Managing Director of the Hunslet Engine Company of Leeds, joined our Society as a Life Member and offered his help. As his Company had taken over the goodwill of Messrs Kerr Stuart when that firm closed down, he expressed particular interest in our locomotive No. 4. Just as Bill, Jim and I had set off for Swindon a year before to secure this engine for the railway, so we had embarked again one bitter winter's day on the longer trek to Leeds. There we discussed this question of boiler repair, and as a result we received from Mr Alcock the most outstandingly generous offer of help which the railway had so far obtained. If, he said, we could arrange to have the locomotive shipped to his works he would carry out the necessary boiler repairs at no charge to the railway. So, after a year's slumber at Pendre, No. 4 had been sent away to Leeds and was promised back in time to bear her share of the summer traffic.

When I came back to the valley the last snows of March had scarcely melted from the crags of Cader Idris, but, within a fortnight, suddenly it was spring again. A mist of green grew each day more dense as buds unfurled like banners in an air that blew warm and scented from the sea. Sodden fields that had lain all winter in shadow now basked in a sun that rode ever higher over the ridges. And each bright day muted the thunder of falling water. Brooks that had shouted in peat-brown spate now ran small and clear, murmuring lazily among their boulders in small voices scarcely to be heard above the bleating of the lambs that flecked the fresh green of every valley pasture. All these portents warned us that it was time to awaken the railway from its hibernation and make good the ravages of the long winter which the searching sunlight revealed all too clearly. The coaches were pulled out of their shed and varnished again, this time inside as well as out, and their underframes, ends and roofs were painted. All the stations were cleaned out and refurbished, while 'the old lady' was given a suit of new green livery appropriately lined out. Just at the end of the previous season old Peter had suddenly been taken so seriously ill that I feared we should never see the old man again. But he had made a remarkable recovery, so to celebrate his return we gave his crossing gates a coat of white paint and embellished them with smart red warning discs in approved railway style. Even the spiders in the dim and dusty recesses of the Wharf office were no longer left in undisturbed possession, for the place was thoroughly cleaned and transformed by fresh distemper. The second room in the Wharf building, hitherto a kind of limbo for odd tools and stores, was also cleaned out, for it had been decided to augment revenue by selling refreshments here and in the disused booking office at Abergynolwyn.

As opening day loomed nearer I began to wonder what this season held in store in the way of alarums and excursions. In some ways it should be less exacting. There were the improvements which had been made, all of which spelt easier working, and if No. 4 fulfilled expectations, there would be two serviceable locomotives available. But by far my greatest asset during this season proved to be the capable and never failing help which I received from my wife who took charge of the booking arrangements and accounts at the Wharf. Without the promise of such help the prospect before me would have been formidable and, indeed, almost overwhelming. For, alas, owing to the demands of his own business, there would be no Chief Mechanical Engineer to preside at Pendre this year. Highly skilled, imperturbable and always ready to cope with any emergency with unfailing good humour, David's presence at Pendre had been immensely reassuring. But now I had to be prepared to grapple alone with any mechanical calamity. Another item on the debit side was the more ambitious time-table. In addition to the previous two trains a day each way from Mondays to Fridays we were now planning a Saturday afternoon service throughout the season and an additional evening service during the height of the season from the last week of July until the first week of September. The time of the afternoon departure was altered from 2.45 to 2.50 to allow more margin for British Railways' dilatory connection, while this train was now scheduled to stand for an hour at Abergynolwyn, returning to the Wharf at 5.50.

During his long vacation from Oxford, which coincided with our peak season, John Snell had volunteered to drive again and with his fireman Gareth Jones would make a relief engine crew. The regular crew this time were to be Bill Oliver and a fireman named Geoffrey Hayes. 'Geoff' was an enthusiastic young member who had paid us a short visit as a volunteer the previous year. As his speech clearly proclaimed, he came from Manchester and with his blue overalls, a wicker 'snapping' basket of enormous size, and a shiny peaked grease cap stuck on the back of his head of curly brown hair he looked every inch the locomotive man. Nor did his looks belie him. Like so many of those who have to do with steam machinery, his walk, and indeed his every movement, was as unhurried and deliberate as the long drawn vowels of his Lancashire accent. But he immediately proved himself an expert fireman with a real pride in the job, and even DOLGOCH in her most cantankerous mood could not make him flustered.

During the week before the season was due to begin, No. 4 appeared at the Wharf on a truck. She was speedily off–loaded by crane and pushed up to the shed by DOLGOCH. To the untutored eye she looked much the same as she had done when she had been first delivered from Machynlleth over a year before except that she now sported a large and prominent mechanical lubricator and carried a new saddle tank painted in flat shop grey. For the superficial work, the painting and furbishing, the fitting of spectacle glasses and name plates had been left for us to complete, but the heart of the locomotive, the boiler, had been entirely rejuvenated at a cost, as it subsequently transpired, of six hundred pounds. Truly a magnificent contribution to the railway.

Unlike the previous year, the start of this season's operations could scarcely have been less auspicious. The official reopening and the beginning of time-table working was to be on Whit Monday, June 1st, but it had been decided to run a train on the previous Saturday afternoon by way of a 'dress rehearsal'. All that sad Saturday the mountains were lost in cloud and veils of thin but extremely wetting rain swept up the valley from the sea. Neverthe-less, DOLGOCH left the Wharf with a full complement of passengers behind her. I did not accompany the train for I was working at Pendre with the object of getting No. 4 ready for steam at the earliest possible moment, so I merely watched her pull away from Pendre and then returned to my work. But little over an hour had elapsed before, to my surprise, I heard the sound of her whistle from the direction of Ty Mawr. Running out into the rain I beheld the sad spectacle of 'the old lady' propelling her train back again. A heavy train, rain on the rust of the little used rails, and the long grass which a warm spring had drawn up to hide the track in places had combined to produce conditions which for the first time had proved altogether too much for her powers of adhesion. She had struggled with great difficulty as far as Cynfal bank but could get no further.

On Sunday the weather was still unsettled, but the soaking showers alternated with long periods of brilliant sunshine which cheered spirits which had been damped in more ways than one by the events of the previous day. Steam was raised in No. 4 and in the late morning I drove her up the line at the head of a train consisting of one coach, the brake-van and a number of wagons which volunteers proposed loading with ballast from Quarry Siding. When we started out I was, I have to confess, in a state of considerable trepidation. For our experiences with No. 3 had left me with no illusions whatever about the possible reactions of strange locomotives to the Talyllyn permanent way. I knew, of course, that No. 4's wheel treads were of the same width as those of DOLGOCH and this was reassuring. Yet I had almost come to believe that, rumbling up and down the valley decade after decade, 'the old lady' had so moulded, or should I say hammered, the permanent way to suit her own inimitable gait that no interloper could hope to follow in her wake without dire consequences. But my confidence in No. 4 grew with every yard of the way. True, she was very prone to slip, for she was the lightest of our four engines and part of that weight, as on No. 3, was carried on trailing wheels. This meant that on our uneven road there were moments when the rear driving wheels lost all adhesive weight and then she would suddenly spin furiously. But apart from this inevitable defect she rode the track in a most reassuring manner, not so lightly and easily as the treacherous SIR HAYDN perhaps, but certainly more comfortably than DOLGOCH.

The result of this trial run was so encouraging that I decided that if the weather was at all doubtful the following morning we would run the inaugural train double-headed. The reopening ceremony was to be performed this time by the President of the Society, Lord Northesk, and it was being broadcast by the B.B.C. so at all costs we must avoid a repetition of Saturday's fiasco. There is an old photograph which shows both TALYLLYN and DOLGOCH at the head of a train but it gives the impression of being a self-conscious and carefully posed show-piece rather than a workaday train, so that a double-headed working might well be a phenomenon without precedent in Talyllyn history. Did it involve too great a risk? That was the vital question. The bridges on the lower part of the line were of so short a span that they would not have to bear any greater weight, but this did not apply to the Dolgoch viaduct. Though the structure of the viaduct had been examined and proved sound, I hesitated to subject it to the rolling weight of two engines and decided it would be wiser to detach the pilot at Brynglas where we would in any case have surmounted the worst of the climb.

The weather on Monday morning, though not actually wet, was unquestionably damp and doubtful, so we decided to put our plan into operation. DOLGOCH, with Bill Oliver in charge, was despatched to the Wharf with the train while after a discreet interval I followed with No. 4. From the point of view of the spectators, the B.B.C. and most of the passengers in the crowded train everything went off without a hitch and with considerable dramatic effect. The Wharf station yard can seldom have presented a more animated scene. Excited people hurried this way and that, microphones were much in evidence and despite the grey day the inevitable cameras were trained on the two engines from every angle, the more so since this was No. 4's first public appearance after long retirement. Finally, after everyone had been persuaded to take their seats in the train, and the President had made a short speech, the signal was given to start. Our whistles answered each other and then the two locomotives forged away under the bridge and up the cutting in a most impressive manner, their exhaust beats combining in a deep, syncopated rhythm and their forceful progress punctuated by the deafening explosions of the detonators which some enthusiast had planted on the line to enliven the proceedings. When the train approached Brynglas it was stopped just short of the station, where, according to plan, No. 4 was detached and run on to the siding. DOLGOCH then took the train on to Abergynolwyn without difficulty while No. 4 returned light to Pendre.

It may all have looked efficient enough yet, as is so often the case on the Talyllyn Railway, things were very far from being what they seemed. No. 4's fire had been banked up and kept in overnight, and in the bustle and excitement of that morning it had not been effectively cleaned. The dire consequences of a dead and dirty fire on this small-boilered locomotive became only too quickly and painfully apparent. For that spectacular start from the Wharf which stirred so many enthusiastic hearts to pleasurable excitement inspired an entirely contrary emotion on the footplate of the pilot as I watched the needle of the steam pressure gauge swing back almost as rapidly as that of a vacuum gauge after a brake application. Almost at once, through no fault of her own, poor No. 4 became almost breathless and a hindrance rather than a help to her partner. If a most ignominious situation was to be avoided it was obvious that the two crews must co-operate closely to save the day. Shouting and signalling back to Bill on the train engine as we rumbled through the cutting towards Pendre, I explained that in an effort to retrieve the situation I was going to leave all the work to him on the easier sections and give him what help I could on the worst banks. In this fashion we reached Rhydyronen, but the state of our fire was too bad to pull round in the little breathing space available and her efforts on Cynfal bank had left No. 4 completely winded. She could scarcely lift herself over the gradient out of the station and the only way we were able to assist was by putting down sand for DOLGOCH. Fortunately 'the old lady' responded nobly to the occasion, but there must surely have been an ironical and slightly malicious grin on the front of her smoke-box as she not only had to pull her heavy train but to push her new partner most of the way from Rydyronen to Brynglas. Our passengers little knew that when No. 4 was uncoupled from the train she had only just enough steam to move herself on to the siding. I feared that as soon as the train was safely out of sight we might have to face the final ignominy of dropping what remained of our fire, for No. 4's normal working pressure was 160 lbs., the water level was out of sight in the bottom fitting of the gauge glass, and I doubted whether her injector could be induced to work on the thirty pounds of steam which was all that remained. However, after a few seconds careful and anxious manipulation the injector consented to pick up. Meanwhile the fire was thoroughly cleaned and remade and before long both water and steam gauges told an altogether more reassuring tale.

It was with considerable amusement that we listened that evening to the B.B.C.'s recorded version of the start of this epic journey. Although it was undoubtedly useful publicity, it contained some sound effects which must have struck the average listener as somewhat peculiar and even slightly alarming. To begin with, DOLGOCH, owing to a blowing blast-pipe joint which was only diagnosed afterwards, had developed a wheeze which sounded for all the world as though a small but vociferous dog had been accidentally shut in the smoke-box and was clamouring for release. After the lady commentator had announced 'They're off', it was this curious noise which was most clearly audible until it was drowned by the explosions of the detonators. As no explanation was given for this deafening fusillade, it must have suggested to those unacquainted with local railway customs that the demonstrative natives were trigger-happy and that Wales was as wild a West as Arizona.

After the opening day, No. 4 was withdrawn from service for a time. For apart from painting and lining out and other finishing work, experience had shown that I must attend to certain mechanical matters before she could give of her best in reliable regular service. For example, a tendency to drop (but not break) springs was cured by modifying their hangers, while an uneven exhaust beat was entirely remedied by carefully resetting the valves. I felt a peculiar regard for this little locomotive and was particularly anxious that she should give a good account of herself. One of a standard type only a mere thirty years old, and by no means an attractive machine to the eye, she lacked DOLGOCH's historical interest and peculiar character. But she appealed to me in a different and much more personal way by recalling nostalgic memories of days now very long past. It may be thought that it is carrying things too far to say that any mere machine is capable of inspiring such a personal feeling as loyalty, yet such was in some sort the case with No. 4. For I had worked beside the men who had built her, many of whom, perhaps, were now dead and gone. Looking at her I could smell once more the sulphurous reek of the foundry where her cylinders had been cast from the roaring, white-hot cupolas, and could hear again the voice of many once familiar machines which had played their part in the fiery and spectacular travail of her birth; the earth-shaking thud of steam hammers that had shaped her connecting rods; the staccato bombardment of pneumatic riveters and, most vociferous of all, the ear-shattering din of a machine popularly known as 'Happy Sam', whose function it was to rivet up both ends of a firebox stay simultaneously. No. 4's wheels had known the rails of the mixed gauge test track where I had once driven a variety of locomotives from a tiny 30 h.p. diesel to an eight-coupled monster with a palatial teak-shuttered cab which was bound for Buenos Aires. So I felt that I owed it to the memory of my old firm to see that this little newcomer should acquit herself well on the Talyllyn. Apart from one mishap which will be recounted later, and excepting the fact that our damp and inferior sand frequently produced a condition of acute constipation in her sanding gear, No. 4 did succeed in upholding the reputation of Kerr Stuart & Company very gallantly. Given a clean, even fire she soon proved herself a much freer and more economical steamer than DOLGOCH, steaming the better the harder she was worked as good locomotives should, and surmounting the long gradients with a proud feather of steam at her safety valves. There was one occasion, too, when double-heading was again resorted to owing to exceptionally bad rail conditions. This time both engines pulled their weight in no uncertain fashion with the result that the ascent of Rydyronen bank from a standing start in the station was a rousing performance as good to hear as to see.

One event in early June which I must confess that I awaited with considerable trepidation was a visit from Colonel D. McMullen, Inspecting Officer of Railways, Ministry of Transport. The effect of publicity can be double-edged, for it was as a result of our efforts in this direction that news of the Talyllyn Railway had eventually filtered through those august ministerial portals in Berkeley Square. I imagine that there may have been some searching of files before it was discovered that the last officials to take a fatherly interest in the behaviour of the Talyllyn Railway were 'Her Majesty's Privy Council for Trade and Foreign Plantations' in 1866. So it was decided that it was high time for an

A devoted band of amateur enthusiasts.' We have a journalist, two manufacturers and an architect in this shot by James Boyd of the early programme of relaying

J.I.C. Boyd

My admiration for this ancient locomotive'. DOLGOCH on a works train early in 1952

John Snell

'The girders of two of our small under-bridges had practically rusted away'. After this finding by Colonel McMullen of the Railway Inspectorate at his June visit, Brynglas bridge was replaced one Sunday by volunteers led by Pop Davies and John Bate, later to be Chief Engineer to the Talyllyn Railway Company

John Snell

Inspecting Officer to visit Towyn and report upon the conduct of affairs there. In the interests of public safety this was a very proper decision, but it was rather a daunting one, for I had a most profound respect for the shrewd efficiency of Her Majesty's Inspectors, and despite our improvements I knew how much had still to be done. It might be possible to beguile our passengers into believing that things were right when in fact they were wrong, but I knew that it would not be merely useless but foolish to attempt to conceal any of our shortcomings from this Sherlock Holmes of the railway world. This certainly proved to be the case. In the course of a rapid but extremely thorough survey, Colonel McMullen missed nothing. Indeed he discovered some things that had escaped us, notably that beneath their concealing timber decking the main girders of two of our small under-bridges had practically rusted away. The worst of the two was the bridge over the stream at the top of Rhydyronen bank. Here Colonel McMullen advised an immediate speed restriction and insisted that the bridge must be strengthened without any delay. Other recommendations were the fitting of point locks and, despite the fact that we worked on a basis of 'one engine only in steam', that the driver should carry a staff on the locomotive. The way in which these and other recommendations were made was entirely constructive and helpful. From his long practical experience Colonel McMullen could and did appreciate our difficulties, so that his attitude could not have been less like that of the popular idea of 'the man from the Ministry' with a brief case stuffed with arbitrary Rules and Orders.

On the Sunday after Colonel McMullen's visit the permanent way department was granted 'total occupation' at Rhydyronen and the weak girders were reinforced by two massive timber baulks. The second offending bridge, at Brynglas, was of greater span. It was reconstructed, again in the course of one Sunday, with sound girders salvaged from a disused bridge at Abergy-nolwyn and brought by rail on bolster wagons to the site. We had two train staffs made, one giving authority to occupy the section between the Wharf and Pendre and the other for the rest of the line. This allowed for movement between the sheds and the terminus at Towyn while the train was up the line, a very necessary provision now that we possessed two workable loco-motives and sometimes had to ring the changes at short notice.

It was indeed fortunate that No. 4 proved a success in service, for although we managed to keep DOLGOCH running to the end she developed various symptoms of mechanical distress which I need not describe but which revealed only too clearly that her efforts of the previous year, when she had borne the burden of traffic alone, had tired 'the old lady' more than we had realised. So she became our stand-by locomotive, enjoying long periods of rest and recuperation in the shed at Pendre while the young partner who had come to her aid in the nick of time handled the larger share of the traffic. Although I had plenty to do to keep both locomotives in working order, the fact that we now pos-sessed a stand-by meant that, except on one occasion which will be described later, mechanical troubles no longer occasioned such acute crises in the motive power department. So it was that during this season, with more trains running and a greater number of passengers travelling, it was the work of the traffic department at the Wharf station which proved the more exacting.

The average railway traveller knows nothing of the activities of the booking clerk. The driver, the fireman and the guard, the stationmaster, inspector and porter, the signalman, the ganger and the wheel-tapper, all these men, to a greater or lesser extent, perform their roles in the public eye whereas for most people the booking clerk is no more than a disembodied hand which scoops up their money and slaps down a small oblong of pasteboard in exchange. There are, of course, many members of a railway's company whose work is done entirely behind the scenes, but of all those who appear on the public stage your booking clerk is the shyest actor. Contact with his public is restricted to a hatchway of the smallest possible dimensions, and even this he often seems reluctant to open until the last possible moment. Because of this excessively retiring disposition little is known about him except that, as a species, he obviously needs plenty of warmth. For on bitter winter mornings after we have sat shivering before the cold grate in the station waiting-room, how tantalising it is to glimpse through his hatchway that heaped up fire of glowing coals which blazes perpetually in his sanctum! Its draught is so great that it sucks the treasury notes out of our frozen fingers and through the pigeon-hole as efficiently as a vacuum cleaner.

I have often pondered upon the reason for this shy seclusion, but now, after two seasons spent at Towyn, I can understand it. For whereas the two old booking offices at Pendre and Abergy-nolwyn were withdrawn from the world in the approved railway fashion, the improvised office at the Wharf afforded no such protection. Across an open counter, the Talyllyn booking clerk and the apparatus of his craft were wholly at the mercy of the public. There was no concealing any error. If his hand failed to fly unerringly to the right compartment in the ticket racks, if he allowed the ribbon of the dating machine to run off its spool, or if his powers of mental arithmetic suddenly deserted him, he must suffer all the agonies of an actor who muffs a vital piece of stage business or forgets his lines. Numerous distractions made such errors easier to commit, for besides issuing tickets, our booking clerk had to be prepared to sell other things such as guides and postcards, to enrol new members for the Society and, most exacting of all, to answer all those questions which the travelling public normally address to ticket inspectors, porters or guards. To answer the same inquiries and to respond with good humour to the same facetious jokes and the same conversational gambits repeated many times daily throughout the season could be as trying to the patience as the most mischievous mechanical perversities of DOLGOCH.

Most of the questions asked concerned the times of the trains, for in this age of universal literacy it is a strange fact that the average railway traveller seems totally incapable of deciphering even the simplest of time-tables, or if he can he refuses to believe what he reads. It has become a profound mystery to me to know how any passenger on British Railways ever succeeds in getting on to the right train, for our little time-table was merely an essay in simple arithmetic compared with the higher algebra of Bradshaw where mysterious and scarcely legible symbols refer the earnest student to some remote page where he discovers such note as: 'Stops to set down only', '3 minutes *earlier* on Saturdays' or 'Will not run after September 1st'. Yet passengers would pore over our time-table for five minutes or more, muttering to themselves the while, before finally giving it up and asking the inevitable question. In self-defence we tried chalking the times on a blackboard but this made very little difference. What un-doubtedly made matters much worse was that, in the mistaken belief that it would prove helpful, we had printed in inset type the times of connecting trains to and from Aberdovey and Barmouth. The effect of this was disastrous. Passengers repeatedly expected us to carry them to these destinations and became quite hurt when we confessed our inability to do so, as who should reproach a shopkeeper for advertising goods which he does not stock.

Even more difficult were those who refused to believe that our trains ran to any time-table at all but thought that they consisted merely of excursions of the 'Any more for the SKYLARK' variety run to suit their convenience. These care-free souls would travel up to Dolgoch or Abergynolwyn, wander off into the wilds and then miss the train back. Eventually they would reappear at the Wharf office, very hot and irate after a long forced march, demanding to know why the train had not waited for them and expecting (but not receiving) a refund on the return halves of their tickets.

In between answering questions and endeavouring to soothe ruffled tempers, the booking clerk was expected to respond suitably to the same jocular remarks interminably repeated. Jokes about the water going off the boil, about the chances of having to get out and push or walk back, about nationalisation and about the Welsh names of our stations which the average passenger made no attempt to pronounce correctly. This last was the most favourite gambit of all, for it is a curious characteristic of the Englishman that whereas he expects every foreigner to master correctly the intricacies of his own language, he will make no effort to return the compliment but insists upon treating all foreign words as an incomprehensible joke. Though all this repartee was invariably well-intentioned, the unfortunate booking clerk may surely be forgiven if, with a set smile on his lips, but murder in his heart, he was occasionally seized with an overwhelming desire to issue all humorists with single tickets to that legendary kingdom beneath the waters of Cardigan Bay.

Even the more seriously minded were at times difficult to deal with tactfully and to send away happy. They usually fell into one of two groups, either the young and enthusiastic:

'I was having a look at the Twatlington Tramway the other day, and I've got a few snaps here which will interest you . . .'

Or the elderly and reminiscent:

'I last travelled on your little railway with my nurse in the year of Queen Victoria's Jubilee, and I well remember . . .'

In other circumstances it would have been very pleasant to discuss the Twatlington Tramway or to know what happened in Jubilee year, but it was extremely difficult to do so when the youth with his 'snaps' or the old man with his memories stood at the head of an impatient queue, when someone was parking a car in the wrong place outside, when a party of children were getting into the wrong carriage and both telephone bells were ringing.

These two instruments, the private and the national, were undoubtedly a great help to the traffic department, but the blessings of modern science are never unmixed and they were all too prone to clamour insistently for attention at the most inconvenient moments. They looked quite impressive, standing side by side on the office desk, so that when, as sometimes happened, it was necessary to use both simultaneously, it was tempting to act the part of a railway tycoon for the benefit of those left waiting at the booking counter. But I doubt whether this act was ever very convincing since it had to be played on a stage whose only lighting was still the old oil lamp with the opalescent glass bowl, and where the two ancient safes, now leaning gently towards each other, were still slowly but surely subsiding through the floor. Moreover, the voices of our two telephones, though both disturbing in their import, were seldom or never connected by any mutual relevance. '*Could* you tell me whether your little train is running?' one would ask in a fruity feminine voice reminiscent of Miss Joyce Grenfell doing one of her impersonations, 'I would like to bring along a party of seventy girls from St Swithin's School.' 'We're having trouble with that so-and-so injector again', the other would reply in hoarse tones of dire foreboding scarcely to be heard above the sounds of escaping steam and somebody hammering. It was tempting sometimes to retire from such an unequal contest and leave the two voices to argue it out.

In the height of the season when the number of potential travellers regularly exceeded the capacity of our train it became extremely difficult for the solitary person in charge at the Wharf to maintain order and prevent the situation from deteriorating into the pandemonium of chaos. Although we never made such a mistake, it would have been fatally easy on these occasions to issue tickets to far more passengers than the train could accommodate. Even the counting of vacant places was apt to be unreliable, for passengers would keep jumping in and out of the train to look at the engine, to take photographs, or to buy a bottle of 'pop' for Johnnie. Then, too, the more artful fathers would plant their wives and families on the train before joining the booking office queue. This played such havoc with our calculations and provoked such bitter scenes of discussion within the queue that we had to make a firm rule that no one should board the train without a ticket. But despite all our efforts to ensure fair play in this daily free-for-all there always seemed to be somebody left behind who considered that he had a grievance, and who refused to accept the fact that lack of sufficient rolling-stock was the one invariable reason for disappointment.

When at length the crowded train pulled out from the Wharf the disappointed stragglers soon melted away and there would fall a sudden, complete and most blessed calm broken only by the measured ticking of the station clock. With a sigh of heartfelt relief the hard pressed booking clerk (assuming he or she had not departed as guard on the train) could then enter up the ticket closing numbers in the Train Book and so find out the number and value of the fares on the train. To this, when the train returned, any bookings made by the guard would be added and a total for the morning or afternoon working struck. A typical page in this Train Book would look like this:

(Date)   TALYLLYN RAILWAY
Afternoon

TRAIN BOOK

Fare		Tickets		No. of Passengers	Fare	Total		
Wharf to:		Open	Close			£	s.	d.
Rhydyronen	S	0056	0057	1	8d.			8
	½S	0033	0035	2	4d.			8
	R	0097						
	½R	0041						
Brynglas	S	0017						
	½S	0012						
	R	0105	0108	3	1/6		4	6
	½R	0024						
Dolgoch	S	0548	0554	6	1/3		7	6
	½S	0101	0102	1	8d.			8
	R	1686	1712	26	2/–	2	12	0
	½R	0915	0920	5	1/–		5	0
Aber	S	0714	0715	1	1/8		1	8
	½S	0219						
	R	2241	2273	32	2/6	4	0	0
	R	0994	1002	8	1/3		10	0
Dogs 2					6d.		1	0
Bicycle 1					1/–		1	0
Parcel to Brynglas								6

Van Bookings

Pen-Dol	R	0514	0516	2	1/9		3	6
	½R	0082	0083	1	11d.			11
Pen-Aber	R	0621	0624	3	2/3		6	9
Dol-Aber	R	0245	0250	5	8d.		3	4
Aber-Whf	S	0322	0323	1	1/8		1	8

Dol–Whf	S	0350	0352	2	1/3	2	6
	½S	0067	0068	1	8d.		8
Cynfal–Whf	S	Paper Ticket	253	1	7d.		7

Total Passengers   102

Train Total   £9   5   1

Loco: No. 4.   Load: 4 and two vans.
Driver: Oliver.   Fireman: Hayes.   Guard: A. N. Other.
Weather: Fine and sunny.
Wharf dep.: 10 late. (Waiting Barmouth connection).
Aber arr.: 5 late.
Aber dep.: 5 late. (Waiting passengers).
Wharf arr.: Time.

In this way each round trip made its page, and thus the Train Book constituted a complete record of the season's working albeit one that was often a masterpiece of under-statement. For only the initiated could appreciate the trials and tribulations that underlay such bald statements as 'Wharf dep 18 late, loco late from shed', or 'Aber arr. 22 late, slipping'.

Heavier pressure on the traffic department compelled us to enlist the help of many more volunteers for guard duties than we had done during the previous year, and almost without exception they proved themselves highly competent. For the job they undertook was a difficult and harassing one, particularly in the height of the season. For these amateur railwaymen had not only to play the part of guard but that of booking clerk as well, and although the volume of booking on the van might be infinitesimal compared with that done in the Wharf office, it must needs be done under peculiarly awkward and distracting conditions. The roles of a booking clerk required to closet himself in that little dark cupboard of an office on the van with its bewildering array of ticket racks, and of a guard who must maintain a constant vigilant watch upon his train were constantly in conflict. But on this

Left: 'A relief crew'. 'John Snell was promoted to driver, a great success, while his place as fireman was filled by Gareth Jones' (*The Times*). Right: 'By far the most harassing freight' (as a general rule). A beautifully behaved group gathered by old No. 1, in this touching shot by Tom Noble

'Improvements went on'. William Jones hedging (in 1953) at Fach Goch

John Snell

A gang prepare to make use of No. 5 for the first time. James Boyd and Tom Rolt sit and Bill Oliver and John Rapley watch other volunteers prepare to go up the line

John Snell

An earlier posed photograph by the *Daily Express* of the general manager, Tom Rolt, and two volunteers pushing a platelayers trolley

problem of divided duty there was never any doubt in my own mind. The safe and efficient running of the train was of far greater importance than any clerical punctilio and the volunteer must remain first and foremost a guard, ever ready to assist the engine crew in any emergency, and constantly on the look out for such potential dangers as children leaning against coach doors which had no safety catches. For although, as Mr Thomas had rightly said, the Talyllyn Railway should not be taken too seriously, on the other hand a train loaded with anything up to a hundred passengers running along a narrow mountain track is no mere toy but a heavy responsibility which it would be fatal to under-estimate. That in the course of two seasons the railway carried over 37,000 passengers without a single case of injury of even the most minor kind shows how capably that care was exercised by all concerned.

Parties of children were by far the most harassing freight, for in all too many cases the masters or mistresses ostensibly in charge of them appeared to be quite incapable of exercising any effective discipline. Whether this chronic incapacity was due to some modern educational theory to do with creating complexes in the young or merely to the abandonment of an unequal struggle I could never be sure. But the uninhibited behaviour of their 'charges' was certainly reminiscent of those demonic little creatures whom Giles or Ronald Searle portray in their cartoons: indeed the scene at the Wharf would sometimes have provided them with excellent copy as with wild cries a horde of children fell upon the train struggling desperately with one another to be first aboard. Had they not been instantly and summarily restrained by our long suffering staff I doubt if by this time much would remain of our ancient coaches except the wheels and under-frames. But no discipline on our part could prevent these children leaving their mark behind them, not only in a litter of paper, leaves and dying flowers on coach floors but in graffiti scribbled and scratched on the woodwork and ceilings of the coaches, on station walls, poster boards and signs. As most of these little hooligans travelled half fare, this was traffic revenue dearly bought. But the nadir of vandalism was achieved by a party of girls of an average age of sixteen or so and of reputedly good education. Unseen by us they completely stripped Dolgoch of its many-coloured rhododendron flowers which so beautified the little station, carried them along the line in armfuls to the viaduct and hurled them down into the ravine below. Episodes such as this, and although it was the worst example it was by no means isolated, scarcely gave us a favourable impression of the educational system of our Welfare State, and revealed the fallacy of the prevailing idea that knowledge is in itself a certain good. Knowledge is certainly power, but without a sense of personal responsibility, without morality and all that we should mean by good manners, it is a very evil power. The small boy who has left his destructive mark on our railway with his pencil and pen-knife will soon learn to command far more potent weapons, but he may remain no less a barbarian for that. He may even become an expert in nuclear physics. It is a daunting prospect.

If these comments upon our holiday freight both adult and juvenile sound a little jaundiced I would redress the balance by saying that with but very few exceptions good will and good humour underlay the faults and the foibles. Had this not been so the work of our Traffic Department would have become quite intolerable. But the fact is that the average Englishman of to-day does not appear at his best when he is on holiday. It is in the environment of his job that he becomes most positively a person, and when he steps out of that environment he leaves much of that personality behind. He puts on an anonymity, and does not, as he believes, assume individuality with his holiday clothes. It is thus the tragedy of the modern world and the prime source of its stresses and strains that work for the majority should have become so uncreative and so destructive to the personality.

The greater these anonymous holiday crowds grew, the more welcome became the sight of familiar local faces on the train. No matter how overwhelming the invasion might be our local passengers were not deterred, while we on our part always found a place for them. Nor must the van ever be so full that room could not be found for the odd sack of coal or chicken meal or for such unwieldy items as a second-hand bedstead or a new hay rake, while such regular institutions as the delivery of the weekly meat ration from Towyn to Llwynwcws Farm must never be forgotten. For the valley clans, Jones, Pugh, Evans and Roberts, were never mere holders of tickets but personalities now well known to us in their natural and workaday context. And because that lonely environment of mountain has so far resisted the great modern steam roller which, in the name of democracy, is flattening all inequalities, even of speech and thought, they retained as strong an individual character as the railway itself. I remember one of them entertaining me in the van one day with the impressions of his one and only visit to London. 'It wouldn't suit me at all', was his summing up. 'There's too many people altogether and all in such a hurry and no friendliness between them. Very wonderful, oh yes, very wonderful, no doubt, but a terrible place indeed.'

Despite our additional locomotive power and the improvements which had been made since the previous year, it was too much to hope that with an augmented train service and a greater volume of traffic we would succeed in running the whole season through without some major breakdown. Past experience had shown that troubles were most likely to occur under the stresses and strains of the traffic peak of late July and August. And sure enough we did have our quota of misfortunes. The old third class coach 'Limping Lulu' was found to have acquired an even more marked limp one day just as the afternoon train was about to depart and had to be detached at Pendre for attention to broken spring bolts. Then 'the old lady', true to form, suffered several partial disintegrations. One of these resulted in the breakage of a cast iron crosshead slipper, and as we had no spare I had to make a temporary repair of the damaged part which I hoped would see the season through. But it was not until the third of September, when the peak of the season was almost past, that serious disaster struck with its usual unpredictable swiftness.

Because I am in no way given to premonitions, it is a curious fact that I should have announced that morning a foreboding that there was going to be some mishap. I had no grounds for thinking so, for it was a fine sunny day and No. 4 had gone up the line as usual with a fairly light train. But when her arrival time came round and she did not appear I became a prey to quite an unreasoning anxiety and when, about ten minutes later, I heard her whistle sound distantly for the Pendre crossing, I experienced a feeling of immense relief. Surely, I said to myself, nothing can happen now. But my relief proved premature. The train came down the gradient in the cutting and ran under the Wharf bridge just as it had done so many hundred times before when suddenly, instead of swinging over the points into the new platform road, there was a lurch, a crash and the locomotive left the rails with all six wheels. It was all over in much less time than it takes to tell, for the train was naturally moving very slowly and Bill had the presence of mind instantly to apply the steam brake. The train remained on the rails and the passengers got out looking, not unnaturally, a little startled by this abrupt and unexpected end to their journey.

I felt certain that this disaster could not have been caused by any defect in our new point-work and a glance at the wreck was sufficient to reveal what had happened. No. 4's trailing wheels were leading at the time. They were of chilled cast iron without tyres, and as they took the curve of the points a large portion of the flange on the outside wheel had broken away with this inevitable result. On examination, the broken piece of flange betrayed an old dark crack of long standing caused, no doubt, by incessant hammering on our rough road but quite undetectable until now.

The situation called for extremely prompt action, first to light up DOLGOCH and get her into steam as soon as possible; second to get the crippled engine back on to the rails. For it would never do for passengers arriving at the terminus for the afternoon train to be greeted by the spectacle of a locomotive leaning at a drunken angle across the line with all her wheels 'on the floor'. Within five minutes of the derailment a good fire was glowing in 'the old lady's' firebox, while down at the Wharf salvage operations had begun. These were greatly helped by No. 4's comparatively light weight. We found that by using two lengths of rail as levers on fulcrums of spare sleepers we were able to lift and swing her, a much speedier procedure than jacking and packing. The accident had happened just before one o'clock and by the time the first passengers began to arrive at a quarter past two they could see nothing amiss. For by that time No. 4 was standing on the loop, her broken trailing wheel coyly concealed from view behind the coaches which were marshalled, as usual, in the platform road. 'Pop', who had proved a tower of strength in this emergency, was still making good the damage caused to the permanent way, but so far as the passengers were concerned this might merely have been a matter of routine maintenance. And as though nothing had ever occurred to disturb an orderly routine, DOLGOCH presently backed down on to the train. She left ten minutes behind schedule, a delay not due to our calamity but to the late running of the British Railways connection.

When the train was out of the section and there were no bystanders left at the Wharf, I began the ticklish job of driving No. 4 from the loop to the repair shop at Pendre. With most of the flange and part of the tread missing from the wheel it was an anxious journey, although it was not until I had to run her over the points and curves in Pendre yard that, despite every care, the trailing wheels twice came off the road and had to be levered on again before the engine was safely in the shop.

I was squatting on the shop floor ruefully surveying the damage, pondering the best way of dealing with it and remembering for the first time that although it was now four o'clock I had had no lunch, when our guardian angel must have woken up with a start and decided it was time that she, too, put in a little overtime. Like the fairy godmother of pantomime she spirited into the shop the very one of the many hundred members of our Society who was best calculated to help in this emergency.

'Do you mind,' said a voice from the doorway behind me, 'if I show my small son round the shed; he's been badgering me to do so all day.' The speaker was at that time a stranger to me although, when I came to look through my old files some time later, I discovered that he was among those who had written to me in the very early days when I had thrown out the first tentative suggestion of trying to maintain the railway. 'Hello!' he went on; 'what's the trouble?' and after surveying the damage with an expert eye, 'If you can take the wheels and axle off and we can get them to my works I can have a new pair of steel wheels pressed on for you.'

This was an outstanding example of the two things which alone made this railway adventure possible: good fortune combined with the goodwill and ready help of sound practical engineers. Your engineer is a craftsman, and between all craftsmen there exists a kind of freemasonry of co-operation. Nowadays, when so much of the work that the engineer is called upon to do is monotonous and unrewarding in the creative sense, the Talyllyn Railway provides a happy contrast and called forth this spirit of co-operation to a remarkable degree. Had it not done so the project would either have remained a cloudy speculation or foundered ignominiously in the first few weeks of life. In this case our friend in need was more than as good as his word. On the day after the disaster I removed the wheels and the following morning we rushed them to a certain pub near Welshpool where they were handed over to his own works transport. Just over a week later the axle was returned to us with new wheels fitted and in the meantime other consequential damage had been made good thanks to the prompt help of other members. As a result No. 4 was back in service less than a fortnight after the disaster.

But for this most fortunate and prompt assistance the season might have ended prematurely and disastrously for we were under no illusions as to the uncertain health of 'the old lady' and every day that No. 4 stood in the shop with her rear end supported by jacks like a cripple on crutches was a day of anxiety. Nor was a serious interruption easily avoided for misfortunes seldom come singly. At midday on the Friday following the accident to No. 4 the bell of the internal telephone at the Wharf rang and my heart sank as I heard John Snell's imperturbable voice begin: 'I regret to report . . .' What could have happened now? When oiling round preparatory to running the loco down to the Wharf he had discovered something seriously amiss with one of DOLGOCH's front springs. I knew only too well after last year's experience what this might involve, so I hurried up to Pendre as quickly as I could after leaving instructions that no bookings should be taken for the afternoon train until I had decided whether the locomotive was fit for service. A very cursory examination was sufficient to reveal that in truth 'the old lady' was very far from well. The spring which David and I had fitted with so much trouble the year before was present and correct and so was the main leaf of its fellow; but that was all; the rest of the off-side spring had broken clean in half. One half had disappeared but the other half remained and was acting as what would be described in motoring circles as a 'reversed quarter-elliptic'.

Now, in what was to be my last month in the service of the Talyllyn Railway, this ancient locomotive confronted me with the most difficult decision of the many I had been called upon to make. And it had to be made quickly, for already passengers were waiting at the Wharf. What some would call discretion and others timidity urged the immediate cancellation of the train, for it was against all the bounds of probability that the broken spring would survive fourteen miles of punishment on our rough road. If it disintegrated the entire train might have to be abandoned some-where up the line until No. 4 was in service again. If this happened the service might have to be suspended for at least a week which would deal a heavy blow to our reputation and mean a serious loss of revenue. Had it been any other day of the week but a Friday I believe these sober counsels would have prevailed, but this was what we had learnt to call 'locals day' and the down morning train had picked up its quota of 'regulars' from Brynglas, Rhydyronen, Cynfal and Fach Goch who were now waiting for us to take them back laden with their week's shopping. It was this fact that turned the scale, this and the consideration that if the desperate gamble did come off there was no service to run on Saturday morning so that we might be able to get DOLGOCH into commission again in time to run that afternoon. If we only succeeded in getting as far as Brynglas, I argued, we would at least have got the locals home, while if the spring did collapse it might be possible to get the train back by jacking up and inserting a wooden block in place of the spring.

So the message 'start booking' went through to the Wharf office while John was told to forget about the running schedule and drive as slowly and carefully as possible. At first I said I would go with him on the train, but on second thoughts I decided it would be sounder policy to accompany the train in my car so that if the worst happened I should be able quickly to summon extra help or arrange emergency transport for our stranded passengers. As on other occasions of crisis, the train departed as usual with its cheerful freight of passengers blissfully unaware of the state of acute anxiety prevailing among the crew and the staff. Perhaps some of the passengers thought it a little peculiar when the old green Alvis which they had seen standing at the Wharf when the train left, appeared again at Rhydyronen, at Brynglas, at the foot of the path at Dolgoch, and yet again at Abergynolwyn. But the ways of railway enthusiasts often appear eccentric to those not so infected and they may have mistaken me for some ardent photographer engaged in taking a series of picture of the train in motion. In fact, of course, at each stop John and I were peering anxiously at the damaged spring on which the fate of the train depended. The valley had never looked more peaceful or more beautiful as it basked in the warm sunlight of that calm late summer day, but as I drove slowly along the road, stopping every now and again, I had eyes only for the white plume of steam, drifting, lifting and dissolving against the green background of the mountains, which told me that DOLGOCH was still on the move. Sound carries far in so narrow and deep a defile, for the mountain slopes make sounding boards as resonant as the walls of an empty room. So whenever I stopped and switched off my engine I could hear the inimitable clank and clatter of her progress and judge from it that John was being as good as his word and taking his time.

That the train succeeded in getting to Abergynolwyn with the abbreviated spring still in place will always strike me as miraculous. Now at any rate if the worst did happen the engine would be at the homeward end of the train and the gradient would favour her. Departure time came and the same procedure began in the reverse direction. This time I did not go up the long and narrow lane to Brynglas but stopped on the main road until steam and sound told me she had started away from that station. I then drove on with the intention of going straight back to Towyn, but when I reached the turning to Rhydyronen a sudden impulse to satisfy myself yet again that all was well made me turn aside once more. I waited on the little station under the pine trees with a feeling of

The doyen of the North West working parties and chairman of the branch, James Boyd, climbs aboard No. 4, cheerful at the end of a long day

'To fetch a load of ballast'. Classic scene by John Adams some years on, at Quarry Siding, from which came all the ballast for the programme of relaying. Volunteers stop to watch a heavy train go up the line

'Assets more valuable than the most up to date equipment'. The working ladies of the railway pose for a ticket buying session at Wharf. Left to right: Peggy Ian and Diana Faulkner; Elizabeth, Dorothy and Diana Boyd

John Adams

growing concern. There was neither sight nor sound of the train. I began to run along the line towards Brynglas, up the steep gradient, over the stream and down the other side. Then I heard the short blast of a whistle followed by the sound of the train starting away very laboriously. I stopped in the 'two foot', and presently DOLGOCH crept very slowly into sight round the curve. There was no need to ask what had happened; I could tell that from the drunken angle of her cab, and as she came past I jumped on to the running plate and held on to the brass rail along her boiler. The old engine was labouring along very painfully, emitting sounds most hideous to the mechanical ear as the rim of the leading driving wheel on the offside ground against the frame, and the coupling rod occasionally hit the slide bar bracket a resounding blow. But we were so nearly home that if she could surmount the short length of rising grade up to Rhydyronen bridge I decided we would try to keep her going. From the moment that the spring had finally disintegrated it became impossible any longer to conceal from the passengers that something was seriously amiss, and each compartment window now framed an agitated or inquisitive head, while worried voices inquired whether they were going to miss their trains back to Barmouth or Aberystwyth. To these we replied with an assurance we were far from feeling. But 'the old lady' struggled gamely on over the summit of the grade so I jumped off when we reached my car and drove back to Pendre where an anxious little group soon gathered on the station platform, waiting for what seemed an eternity. But it must have been a far more anxious time for John, nursing his crippled engine slowly over this last long lap with the knowledge that at any moment such unnatural stresses and strains might cause some far more dire calamity. Old Peter was the first to see her, knowing from long experience the precise spot between trees and high hedges where the first glimpse was possible. 'There she is,' he called excitedly, gazing up the valley with narrowed eyes. 'She's coming up to Hen-dy bridge now'. He chuckled. 'She'll be alright. Lord bless you, yes; he's a good lad is John . . . aye, aye.' Ten minutes later DOLGOCH staggered into Pendre and brought her train to a stand at the platform barely half an hour behind time. The last gamble had come off, but it had been a very close call.

After my account of the efforts of David and myself when similarly engaged, I can leave to the imagination the scene which was enacted, with frequent outbursts of blasphemy, in Pendre shed that night and all the next morning. Suffice it to say that 'the old lady' reappeared with a new front spring fitted in time to run the service on the following afternoon. So there were no sad blank pages in the Train Book after all; only a brief entry at the foot of the page reserved for Friday, September 5th, which read: 'Arr Pendre 29 late and there terminated; o.s. front spring broken.'

A week later EDWARD THOMAS emerged from the repair shop to the timely rescue of a somewhat exhausted and decrepit DOLGOCH, and a second successful season drew to an uneventful close. Once again the service had been maintained with a regularity which was, on the whole, exemplary. In fair weather or foul, day after day from bluebell to blackberry time the trains had again run to and fro beneath the frowning ridges of Ffridd Brynglas and Mynydd Pentre and over the Dolgoch ravine on their lofty viaduct. Day after day their whistles, the shrill cry of DOLGOCH or the deeper note of EDWARD THOMAS, had echoed from mountain to mountain and men had looked up from their work in the fields to watch them pass, the light glinting on green livery and the brave show of polished brasswork. They had hauled this season no less than 22,000 passengers over the seven miles of narrow track and the revenue had climbed up to four figures. This had been achieved with a regular staff whose numbers had varied from three at the beginning of June to seven at the season's peak and with the assistance of a relatively small but absolutely invaluable band of volunteers, most of whom had already proved their worth the previous year. The handicaps of worn permanent way, ancient rolling-stock and primitive equipment could never have been so triumphantly overcome and the service maintained contrary to all the laws of probability had it not been for two assets more valuable than the most up-to-date equipment – the enthusiasm and love of the job which inspired staff and volunteers alike. It was this that impelled them to work seven days a week and anything up to twelve hours a day, sometimes with scarcely a break for meals, without any talk of overtime or word of complaint. Our small company was recruited from many widely separated walks of life; undergraduates, shopkeepers, clergymen, engineers, railwaymen and schoolmasters worked side by side with us, and neither among volunteers nor staff was there any hierarchy or nice distinctions. The words 'That's not my job' have not been heard yet on the Talyllyn Railway. If a job had to be done it was done by whoever was available however menial, dirty and arduous it might be.

The Talyllyn Railway, some may say, has become a worn out anachronism in this age of the jet plane and the atom bomb into which it has strayed. Surely, then, so much time, money and energy could have been expended to some better purpose? To this I would reply with another question: What other and more fruitful fields has the planned state left open for individual intitiative and creative enterprise to till to-day? Very few. With every year that passes there is less fertile ground left and it is a dreary, ill-nourished crop which sprouts in the state-owned fields. False quantitative standards of equality and uniformity imposed in the name of democracy; the false equation of mere size with efficiency which assumes that the larger the organisation the better it must be; these things run counter to the grain of human nature and lead to damnation and the dark night of the spirit. Our trains must all be of one colour now (except on the Talyllyn) and are to be hauled by 'standard' locomotives of questionable merit. Our motor cars all look alike, indeed almost everything we use, wear or eat must conform to the same shoddy common denominator of suburban values. Our trains and our buses, like the aeroplanes which roar overhead, no longer possess the positive character of local institu-tions. Like the current at the switch or the water from the tap they have become 'public services' ruled by 'them' – unknown officials who might dwell upon a different planet, so top-heavy is the hierarchy of officialdom and so remote from the local commu-nities which it ostensibly exists to serve. It is against this imposed and world-levelling order that the creative individual is bound to fight, not only for standards of truth and of beauty, but for his own survival. For if it is not so opposed there can be no end to this desolation until the last hill has been bulldozed flat and the last crooked lane made straight.

The Talyllyn Railway is one of the very few lanes which have not been made straight or bull-dozed off the map. In thirteen years' time it will be a hundred years old. Will 'the old lady' be able to steam up the valley in 1966 to celebrate that centenary? Who can say? It is hard to swim against the current of the age although it is better to do so than to be swept away without making some effort to stem such a tide. But the harsh fact is that the railway is unremunerative as I realised all too clearly when I observed the catastrophic effect upon my bank balance of two summers spent at Towyn. Because it can earn traffic revenue only during a short summer season, the railway can only be restored to good order and adequately staffed with the aid of heavy subsidies from the Preservation Society.

It is, of course, arguable that when economic or social change threatens any institution with extinction it should be left to die because attempts to preserve it, however well-intentioned, are but nostalgic kickings against the pricks of change and can only succeed in embalming a corpse from which the spirit has flown. There is so much truth in this argument that in any other age but this it would be unassailable. But we are moving rapidly towards a new Dark Age where evils of unprecedented power threaten the whole world. And when the house is afire the instinct to save something of value from the blaze is too strong to be denied. All those things which represent human dignity and individual liberty, and which affirm that man is spirit as well as flesh are imperilled by this new Dark Age. Are we then to stand passively by and see them consumed? Moreover, even upon the more mundane level of pounds, shillings and pence it is no longer logical to condemn any worth-while institution to extinction on economic grounds when the prevailing notion of economy enables State Corporations to squander with complete impunity millions of public money upon projects more fantastic than any South Sea Bubble.

It may be thought that I am seeking to magnify out of all true proportion the significance of our effort to preserve one small railway in a remote valley of the Welsh mountains. But the Talyllyn Railway is not simply an engineering museum piece; it is a local institution and as such it has become a part of Wales and of Welsh life. As such it is a lonely witness to the fact that the work of the engineer is not necessarily either destructive or of a soul-destroying uniformity. That, on the contrary, he once enriched with diversity the topography of these islands of ours just as surely as other and older craftsmen have done before him.

Wordsworth, Ruskin and many lesser stars in the Victorian firmament vilified the new railways when their cuttings and embankments were raw gashes of naked earth and rock. But they could not see the shape of things to come, whereas we who look back now see that our railways were the last great contribution of the engineer-craftsman to the English scene. In a space of time surprisingly short the railway engineer built up traditions of craftsmanship, of service and pride in the job which only our seaways could surpass. The crested liveries of his locomotives, aglint with the pride of burnished copper, brass and steel, soon became identified with the territories they served. As surely as local speech they evoked the Downland chalk, the Devon Combe, or the long levels of the Norfolk Fen. And what men they are who, out of early, faded photographs, look down at us like monarchs from the footplates of these splendid machines! Hard-hatted and heavily be-whiskered, proud in their suits of white cords, these are not the first machine minders but the last Commoners of England, men who brought to the railways the qualities of an older tradition which our Welfare State has lost and forgotten. Nor was that tradition confined to the footplate. The local line inspired fierce local patriotism. The village railway station soon became an institution like the church and the pub, while its master, gold-braided and flower in button-hole, joined the parson, the squire and the publican in the ranks of village worthies.

When the old railways were amalgamated into four great Companies, two of them hopelessly unwieldy, their traditions suffered a heavy blow. Now 'nationalisation' is administering the *coup de grâce* to a conception of loyalty and service, to a sense of vocation which now lives only in the memories of the older railwaymen. The brighter that memory the more bitter and the more disheartening their lot is becoming, for railways are no longer run by railwaymen and engineers but by Civil Servants and economists whose ruling principle is that before any improvement can be sanctioned a financial economy must first be proved on paper. So your railwayman struggles on, throttled in red tape and fighting a losing battle with obsolete or worn out equipment. No wonder if he no longer flaunts a flower in his button-hole; no wonder if his locomotives no longer gleam and glitter; no wonder if the train that was once as punctual as the Greenwich time-signal now runs forty minutes late. One day there will be no one left to care.

In this ancient kingdom of Gwynedd, under the shadow of Cader Idris we have striven against odds not merely to preserve a railway but to keep alive a spark of that fine tradition which flourished so richly when the Talyllyn line was born. Is it not worth cherishing? If only enough people think so, then the railway can be completely restored and its future assured. But even if the worst should happen and our venture fail for lack of adequate support, at least a gesture has already been made and by no means an idle or a fruitless one. Certainly in the last two years the Talyllyn Railway has given pleasure to thousands, a new sense of purpose to those who have joined our Society, and to me good companions and an adventure which I shall remember all my days.

From the author's album. Two scenes showing the start of the railway adventure. On the back of the left one he wrote, 'A sight we hope to see again'.

A railway revived. By AGM day 1953 barely two years on, the familiar scene at Wharf shows no less than three engines in steam, and platform and new track. Left to right: 'the old lady', the heroine of the adventure, No. 3 SIR HAYDN, and No. 4 EDWARD THOMAS, who is hurrying up the passengers

J.J. Davis